PATRICK McNEIL, creator of designmeltdown.com

THE WEB DESIGNER'S
IDEA BOOK

TYPE · Blog · Forum · Event · E-Commerce · Free Script · Church · Personal · Design Firm · Photography Portfolio · Web Hosting · Web Services · Web Software · DESIGN STYLE · Retro · Minimalist · Super-Clean · Distressed · Three-Dimensional · Sketchy · Collage · Illustrated · Photographic · Giant Type · Let the Art Speak · THEME · Nature · Food · Old Paper · Grass · Wood · Clouds · Splatters · Workplace · Print Imitation · Location-Based · Extreme Theme · COLOR · Pink · Red · Orange · Yellow · Green · Blue · Purple · Brown · Black · Gray · White · Black & White · Pink & Blue · Blue & Green · Bold · Muted · ELEMENT · Icons · Dates & Calendars · Rounded Corners · Folded Corners · Rays · Tags · Crests · Badges · Stripes · Ornate Elements · Ornate Backgrounds · Gradients · Shine · STRUCTURE · Horizontal Scrolling · Zoom In · Atypical Navigation · Tabs · Three Buckets · Modules · Tiny · One Page · Massive Footers · Atypical Layout · Hybrid

the ultimate guide to themes, trends and styles in website design

HOW BOOKS

Cincinnati, Ohio
www.howdesign.com

For more fine books from F+W Publications, visit www.fwpublications.com.

3 12 11 10 09   6 5 4 3 2

Distributed in Canada by Fraser Direct, 100 Armstrong Avenue, Georgetown, Ontario, Canada L7G 5S4, Tel: (905) 877-4411. Distributed in the U.K. and Europe by David & Charles, Brunel House, Newton Abbot, Devon, TQ12 4PU, England, Tel: (+44) 1626 323200, Fax: (+44) 1626 323319, E-mail: postmaster@davidandcharles.co.uk. Distributed in Australia by Capricorn Link, P.O. Box 704, Windsor, NSW 2756 Australia, Tel: (02) 4577-3555.

Library of Congress Cataloging-in-Publication Data

McNeil, Patrick.
  The Web designer's idea book : the ultimate guide to themes, trends, and styles in website design / Patrick McNeil.
      p. cm.
  Includes bibliographical references and index.
  ISBN 978-1-60061-064-6 (pbk. : alk. paper)
  1. Web sites--Design--Case studies. 2. Web sites--Directories. I. Title.
  TK5105.888.M42 2008
  006.7--dc22

                                                          2008019480

All color palettes courtesy of COLOURlovers.com © 2007.
Original text on page 26 courtesy of Casey Barthels © 2007.
Original text on page 177 courtesy of Mel Hogan © 2007.

Edited by Amy Schell
Designed by Grace Ring
Production coordinated by Greg Nock

PATRICK McNEIL, creator of designmeltdown.com

THE WEB DESIGNER'S IDEA BOOK

the ultimate guide to themes, trends and styles in website design

DEDICATION

For my biggest fan, my mom Alyce

ABOUT THE AUTHOR

Patrick McNeil is a freelance web developer and the creator of www.design-meltdown.com. His diverse interests have merged web technology and design, resulting in work that touches everything from high design to hardcore programming.

Ultimately, his love for design, inspiration and sharing knowledge has fueled his passion for running Design Meltdown, where he has cataloged and observed web design trends over the last few years. It is this passion that led to the creation of this very book.

ACKNOWLEDGMENTS

This book would never have been possible if it were not for the hundreds of designers pouring their hearts into their work and making such a feast of beautiful web design. I thank them all for their inspiring work. I also owe a debt of gratitude to the loyal readers of Design Meltdown who have continually affirmed the need for resources such as this. Many thanks go to the fine people at F+W Publications for taking on this project and making this all come together. Most of all I want to thank my wife Angela for her many hours of listening to me drone on about web design, and my mother, who is perhaps my biggest fan, reading every last word I produce. She also helped pull together the mountain of release forms needed to make the book possible.

TABLE OF CONTENTS

WORD FROM THE AUTHOR

Cataloging web design is a dangerous business that starts with a few obvious topics and soon leads to hundreds of categories and thousands of samples. This book represents two years of just such methodical activity. Inspired by the work of Steven Heller in his book *Genius Moves: 100 Icons of Graphic Design*, I searched for inspiration in modern web design patterns by creating the website Design Meltdown. The result of this experiment exceeded my expectations. The inspiration I found in these random groupings snowballed into the book that is before you today.

To say that it is a challenge to create a current book about the web is an enormous understatement. By the time this book is published, countless samples will have changed while others will have disappeared completely. This is to be expected. In fact, it is the web's continuous growth and change that appeals to many web designers and keeps the industry exciting. The irony of such change is that it creates an endless need for resources like this book.

I like to think of this book as a snapshot in time. It captures the web as it exists in 2008, showcasing the very best we have to offer at this time. The inclusion of certain topics and the exclusion of others reflects the status of the industry and will hopefully serve as a reference point in years to come. I like to think that web design, like print design, can be nostalgic, and that old styles can return from the grave to find new life. The industry has gotten to a point where it is truly respected as a legitimate platform for commerce, and more interestingly, design. As a result, the quality has improved immensely. I hope we do not look back on this era's web design with disdain—as we sometimes do the earlier years of the Internet—but instead appreciate the works that have been created and allow them to re-inspire us to shape the future.

—Patrick McNeil, July 2008

01

Blog Forum Event E-Commerce Free Script Church Personal Design Firm Photography Portfolio Web Hosting Web Services Web Software

SITES BY TYPE

The selected site types presented in this book barely scratch the surface of possibilities. In fact, one could easily create an entire book based on the cataloging of sites by their industry or purpose. The selection of topics here, such as web services, software and the ever-present need for web hosting, serves to represent some of the most active segments of the online world. From portfolios and blogs to church sites, these categories showcase some of the finest sites in each segment, and effectively capture exciting new areas of development right now.

01
SITES BY TYPE

Blog Forum Event E-Commerce Free Script Church Personal Design Firm Photography Portfolio Web Hosting Web Services Web Software

BLOG

An entire book could be written on beautiful blog design, so it seems absurd to present only a few examples here. Unfortunately, the scope of this particular book requires me to limit these examples to a few incredibly beautiful ones. The biggest challenge for blog designers is to create a fresh, new design that isn't stuck in a basic blog default template.

One design pattern that works well is to highlight the most recent post on the homepage so it stands out. A remarkable example of this is North x East. This beautifully crafted blog essentially has the title of the most recent post displayed prominently in the main banner. This is one of the most distinct and effective implementations of this particular style. It appeals to repeat visitors by making the most recent post easy to find. Instead of facing the overwhelming task of choosing from a list of interesting titles, even new users are encouraged to dig deeper on this site by starting with the suggested post.

Another nice example of the highlighted post is on Veerle Pieters's blog, which displays the most recent post on the left and a list of previous posts next to it. A short excerpt, a date icon and a large title all help to set the highlighted post apart. Another nice feature of this blog is that it focuses more on the categories of the posts than the order in which they were written. This topic-oriented organization suits the site's content and readers. This is a subtle distinction, but it is certainly different from the default configuration of most blogging engines.

Yet another example of this approach is Eleven3. The primary brand of the site takes up the majority of the screen when the site initially loads. What follows is standard blog content, except that, again, the newest post is emphasized. This unique approach meets the traditional needs of a static sales-oriented site with the fresh content of a thriving blog.

The final twist on this pattern is to display the full content of the most recent post. Design 2.0 does this. Users can easily read the new content without having to click past the homepage. Interestingly, this minimal approach is perfectly aligned with the overall minimal style of the blog.

Ultimately, the goal of blog design is to capture new visitors while rewarding repeat users. Creating an easy-to-consume design is a key piece of the puzzle. Making a distinct and beautiful design is certainly another. These samples have done both.

http://veerle.duoh.com

http://northxeast.com

http://www.eleven3.com

http://design2-0.com

http://www.thedesignedtree.com

http://www.jrvelasco.com

http://aialex.com

http://www.obeattie.com

http://contactsheet.de

http://tatteredfly.com

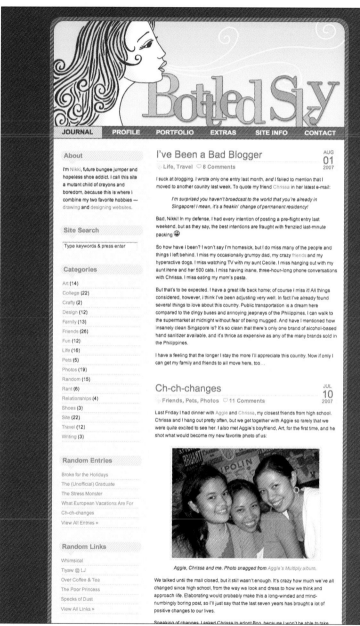

About

I'm Nikki, future bungee jumper and hopeless shoe addict. I call this site a mutant child of crayons and boredom, because this is where I combine my two favorite hobbies — drawing and designing websites.

Site Search

Type keywords & press enter

Categories

Art (14)
College (22)
Crafty (2)
Design (12)
Family (13)
Friends (26)
Fun (12)
Life (16)
Pets (5)
Photos (19)
Random (15)
Rant (6)
Relationships (4)
Shoes (3)
Site (22)
Travel (12)
Writing (3)

Random Entries

Broke for the Holidays
The (Unofficial) Graduate
The Stress Monster
What European Vacations Are For
Ch-ch-changes
View All Entries »

Random Links

Whimsical
Tiyaw @ LJ
Over Coffee & Tea
The Poor Princess
Specks of Dust
View All Links »

I've Been a Bad Blogger

AUG 01 2007

Life, Travel ⬤ 8 Comments

I suck at blogging. I wrote only one entry last month, and I failed to mention that I moved to another country last week. To quote my friend Chrissa in her latest e-mail:

I'm surprised you haven't broadcast to the world that you're already in Singapore! I mean, it's a freakin' change of permanent residency!

Bad, Nikki! In my defense, I had every intention of posting a pre-flight entry last weekend, but as they say, the best intentions are fraught with frenzied last-minute packing 😊

So how have I been? I won't say I'm homesick, but I do miss many of the people and things I left behind. I miss my occasionally grumpy dad, my crazy friends and my hyperactive dogs. I miss watching TV with my aunt Cecile. I miss hanging out with my aunt Irene and her 500 cats. I miss having inane, three-hour-long phone conversations with Chrissa. I miss eating my mom's pasta.

But that's to be expected. I have a great life back home; of course I miss it! All things considered, however, I think I've been adjusting very well. In fact I've already found several things to love about this country. Public transportation is a dream here compared to the dingy buses and annoying jeepneys of the Philippines. I can walk to the supermarket at midnight without fear of being mugged. And have I mentioned how insanely clean Singapore is? It's so clean that there's only one brand of alcohol-based hand sanitizer available, and it's thrice as expensive as any of the many brands sold in the Philippines.

I have a feeling that the longer I stay the more I'll appreciate this country. Now if only I can get my family and friends to all move here, too...

Ch-ch-changes

JUL 10 2007

Friends, Pets, Photos ⬤ 11 Comments

Last Friday I had dinner with Aggie and Chrissa, my closest friends from high school. Chrissa and I hang out pretty often, but we get together with Aggie so rarely that we were quite excited to see her. I also met Aggie's boyfriend, Art, for the first time, and he shot what would become my new favorite photo of us:

Aggie, Chrissa and me. Photo snagged from Aggie's Multiply album.

We talked until the mall closed, but it still wasn't enough. It's crazy how much we've all changed since high school, from the way we look and dress to how we think and approach life. Elaborating would probably make this a long-winded and mind-numbingly boring post, so I'll just say that the last seven years has brought a lot of positive changes to our lives.

Speaking of changes, I asked Chrissa to adopt Boo, because I won't be able to take

http://bottledsky.com

http://www.ashhaque.com/blog

http://www.quicksprout.com

01
SITES BY TYPE

Blog **Forum** Event E-Commerce Free Script Church Personal Design Firm Photography Portfolio Web Hosting Web Services Web Software

FORUM

Forum design can be difficult. A balance must be struck between the need to be unique and the need to meet user assumptions about how forums function. It is clearly a bad idea to disorient visitors by changing the standard forum layout too much. However, the forum will not stand out in the default design and layout, which is anything but beautiful. Some forums need to stand out more than others, but all forums need to be easy to use. Most forum applications are loaded with features that users don't need or understand. The designs selected for this chapter have reduced the forum to its most critical elements while managing to produce beautiful sites.

Of these samples the Designs Advice forum stands out the most. It sticks with some of the traditional interface elements but still manages to brand the

system effectively. Most of the extra, unneeded items have been removed. This cleans up the site and makes the wealth of information it contains far easier to consume. The site successfully balances the need for a unique brand and a user-friendly format.

The price of success is more success. How can an effective forum design stand the test of time and thousands of posts? What happens when it contains so many posts that no human could ever consume them all? This is precisely the problem that Designers Talk faces. At the time of this writing, this general forum has over seventy thousand posts. On top of this, it contains over twenty-five different forums. The key to this forum site's success is how the design cuts through the clutter by suggesting a hierarchy of information. Instead of

presenting a ton of elements with the same weight, the designers made the important elements more noticeable. Because of this, it is surprisingly easy to scan the long list of forums to find one of interest. Once inside a forum, the layout is amazingly clean and easy to read. Again, skimming for a topic of interest couldn't be easier. Together, reasonably sized text and a bold color create the user-friendly interface.

One of the biggest potential pitfalls of any forum design is going with the default skin. Most forums contain too much information. Let's face it—if a forum is reasonably active, will anyone care what the last post date was? Assume that users want to read something, and help them find topics of interest by creating a design that is easy to dive into.

http://designsadvice.com

http://www.designleague.de

http://www.designerstalk.com/forums

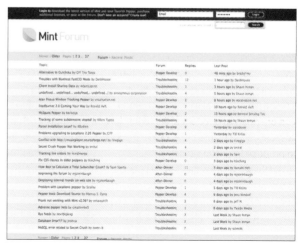

http://haveamint.com/forum

http://www.typophile.com/forums

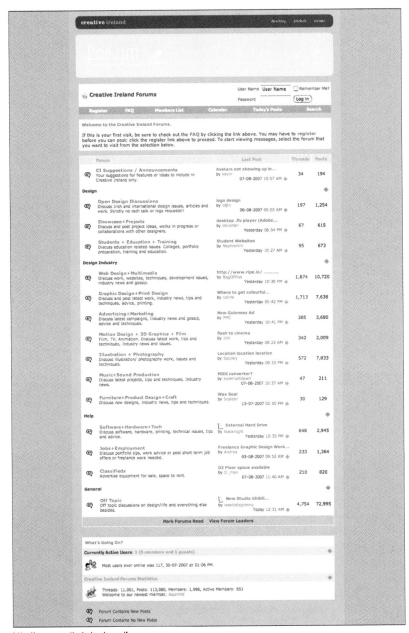

http://www.creativeireland.com/forums

01

SITES BY TYPE

Blog   Forum   **Event**   E-Commerce   Free Script   Church   Personal   Design Firm   Photography   Portfolio   Web Hosting   Web Services   Web Software

EVENT

The main obstacle that event sites face is that they have two audiences: those who want to attend a show and those who want to perform in a show. The importance of each type of audience varies depending on the event. Some events have a predetermined schedule of speakers, while others, like art shows, recruit participants. I suppose it comes down to this: Do the people in the show pay their way in, or are they paid to be there?

The most obvious way to make a successful event site is to think literally. As with any site, it is wise to brand it to the appropriate demographic. Sites like Future of Online Advertising have made great efforts to appeal to young, hip web owners. Its trendy green, blue and brown palette shows that the firm is in touch with web trends, which communicates the fact that it does, indeed, know the future of online advertising. Of course, the list of featured speakers communicates this as well, but the design has its impact first, making it critical.

Another major obstacle that the event site faces is that it inevitably becomes outdated. It is usually clear when a site will become obsolete, and this tends to hinder committees from lavishing it with funds. This makes the extraordinary designs in this category even more impressive.

http://www.futureofonlineadvertising.com

http://ostrava.rails.cz

http://2007.dconstruct.org

http://markandvelma.enews.org

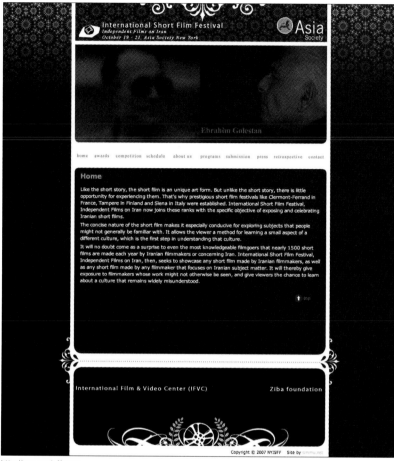

http://www.nyisff.com

http://www.eurobands.us

http://www.starlighteventdesign.com

http://www.expo-canada.com

http://www.witpage.com

01
SITES BY TYPE

Blog Forum Event E-Commerce Free Script Church Personal Design Firm Photography Portfolio Web Hosting Web Services Web Software

E-COMMERCE

Few of us will ever get the opportunity to work on an e-commerce site the size of Amazon. There are many medium-sized e-commerce sites that employ developers, but ultimately the most potential for creative and beautiful presentation lies with small, niche sites.

Large sites tend to die in committees, where groups of people determine how things will work and look. In many ways this is great. Amazon certainly has a distinct look, is accessible and has some advanced features, but it has a bare-bones functional design.

Small e-commerce sites present an awesome opportunity to focus on the product and market. Consider Amazon, whose customer base includes just about anyone using a computer. They sell books,

music, computers and even groceries. That is an extremely broad market. Now consider a site like Loop De Lou. Because they have a small niche of products that a specific demographic will be shopping for, they can create a much more focused design that addresses the style expectations of the market. The fashionable design will likely appeal to people who are shopping for custom stationery.

This opportunity to create a focused marketing plan is empowering. It is easier and more fun to design within constraints. Too little focus leaves you floundering for a direction that is universally appealing. Whether your market is teenaged girls or retired seniors, embrace your demographic and capitalize on what appeals to them.

Tools like Yahoo! Store and eBay make it all too easy to use a default template. In most cases, however, the effectiveness of a site is directly related to the effectiveness of its design. These samples all rise above the rest and stand as superb inspiration for what can be accomplished on an e-commerce site.

Amid all this fun and exciting branding, it is important to remain ever-mindful of the customer. Above all, an e-commerce site should have a clear purchasing process. Nothing kills an e-commerce site like a confusing checkout process. A careful blend of branding and practicality is what makes these sample sites outstanding.

http://www.loopdelou.com

http://www.paper-cloud.com

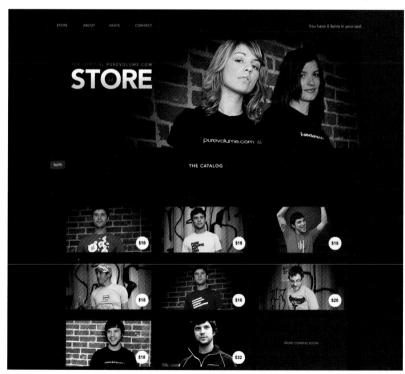

https://store.purevolume.com

http://www.junglecrazy.com

http://www.bloomingdirect.com

http://www.lloydfarms.com

http://www.concretehermit.com

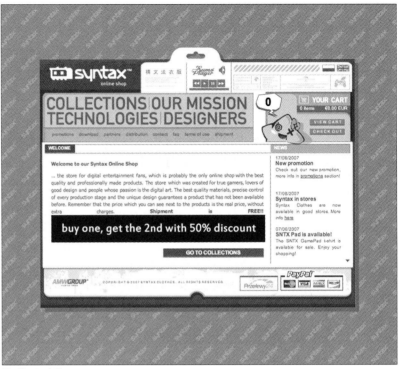

http://syntaxclothes.com

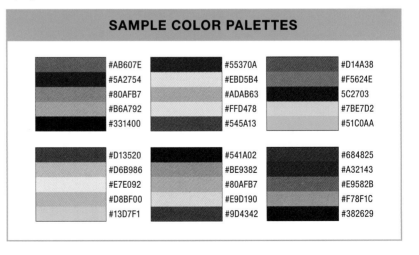

SAMPLE COLOR PALETTES

#AB607E	#55370A	#D14A38
#5A2754	#EBD5B4	#F5624E
#80AFB7	#ADAB63	5C2703
#B6A792	#FFD478	#7BE7D2
#331400	#545A13	#51C0AA
#D13520	#541A02	#684825
#D6B986	#BE9382	#A32143
#E7E092	#80AFB7	#E9582B
#D8BF00	#E9D190	#F78F1C
#13D7F1	#9D4342	#382629

01

SITES BY TYPE

Blog   Forum   Event   E-Commerce   **Free Script**   Church   Personal   Design Firm   Photography   Portfolio   Web Hosting   Web Services   Web Software

FREE SCRIPT

It is simply incredible how much work people will put into giving things away. All of these sites offer killer sets of tools at the low, low price of absolutely nothing. You would hardly believe this is the case when looking at these sites. It seems like there must be some sort of string attached, but amazingly there isn't.

It is really cool to see how seriously people take the tools they have created. They present them on beautiful sites in a way that elevates the tools to a higher level. Presentation has a huge impact on how something is perceived; good presentation enhances the expected quality of an item. Why does this matter? The community benefits from the hard work of these free script site designers, and I imagine the designers view this as a way to give back to all the people they have learned from.

Free script sites need a pretty wrapper to attract developers. Quite simply, most people judge a book by its cover. If a site for some JavaScript library is hacked up with nasty ads, it is probably safe to assume that the site's lack of self-respect points to a junky code. However, if a beautifully designed site is devoid of ads, it is likely that the owners genuinely love their product and are gladly giving it away.

One interesting thing to note is that any call to action seems to be of secondary importance on these non-commercial sites. Instead, they focus on explaining what their products do. Take the videoMaru site, for example. The product demo takes precedence over the download link. In any case, the work put into these sites is simply an example of the work put into the code itself.

http://www.flashden.net/videomaru

http://www.mochikit.com

http://www.swfir.com

http://script.aculo.us

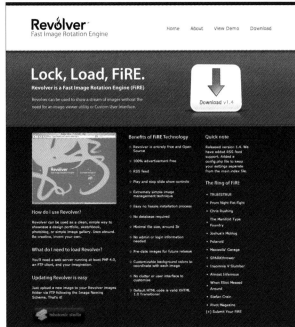

http://www.tubatomic.com/revolver

http://www.prototypejs.org

http://yurivish.com/yshout

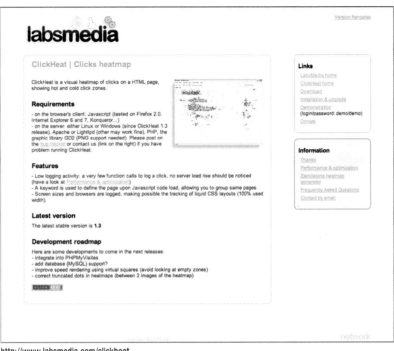

http://www.labsmedia.com/clickheat

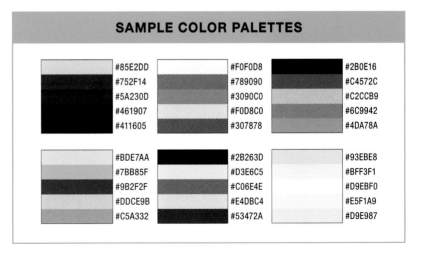

SAMPLE COLOR PALETTES

#85E2DD	#F0F0D8	#2B0E16
#752F14	#789090	#C4572C
#5A230D	#3090C0	#C2CCB9
#461907	#F0D8C0	#6C9942
#411605	#307878	#4DA78A

#BDE7AA	#2B263D	#93EBE8
#7BB85F	#D3E6C5	#BFF3F1
#9B2F2F	#C06E4E	#D9EBF0
#DDCE9B	#E4DBC4	#E5F1A9
#C5A332	#53472A	#D9E987

01
SITES BY TYPE

Blog Forum Event E-Commerce Free Script **Church** Personal Design Firm Photography Portfolio Web Hosting Web Services Web Software

CHURCH

The level of quality found in these church sites is rather impressive, especially considering the fact that few volunteer organizations have such wonderful sites. And this is just a small selection of the dozens of spectacular church websites. It is always nice when passionate individuals apply their talent to benefit low-revenue or pro bono sectors.

What fascinates me about these examples is how the personality of each church site reflects the personality of its members. A church, like any organization, has to sell itself. Using its site design to connect with its target demographic is an effective way to do this. Sure, a church is typically open to anyone, but it tends to attract like-minded people. When a church's website clearly reflects its members, it effectively connects with the people who are most likely to stick around. In the business world this is called customer retention, but it seems brash to apply traditional business terms to religion, even if it is in the business of saving souls!

My point is that church web design is about more than being trendy. It is about connecting with the heart of the organization and presenting it accurately and attractively. This is not so different from any other website, but the purpose is just a little more obvious and necessary.

A great example is the Vintage Church site. It has an expressive, hip and, dare I say, cool feel. The landing page alone reflects a church that is rooted in modern aesthetic, which leads viewers to assume that the church practices modern worship and preaching. In contrast, Northstar Church has a far more conservative site. I don't know anything about this church, but its site seems to be geared towards young families. My point is that a website reflects personality. Designers are in control of this and must use appropriate imagery, color and style to reflect the church accurately.

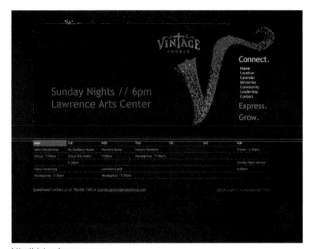

http://vintagelawrence.com

http://www.kaleohouston.com

http://www.northstarchurch.cc

http://rooftop.org/

http://www.launchachurch.com

http://www.elevation.cc

http://www.parkviewbaptist.net

http://www.nwoods.org

SAMPLE COLOR PALETTES

#C0C060	#D86649	#333333	#604818	#301818	
#A8A848	#EC995A	#0077CC	#D8D8A8	#C04800	
#909048	#FFB473	#FF0044	#483018	#F0D8A8	
#A8D8F0	#C98649	#EEDDDD	#909060	#FF69A5	
#787830	#8B5819	#1177CC	#F0C0A8	#303048	

#B15500	#01002B	#A73831	#000000	#A24E12	
#C98444	#486060	#794C2B	#062253	#EBAB4F	
#E2C5A9	#78A8C0	#73653E	#3078C0	#99280B	
#5A3E19	#D8D8A8	#FFF1D4	#9CC4E4	#472A14	
#6D491B	#C00000	#EEE5E0	#F0F0F0	#FFAE47	

01
SITES BY TYPE

Blog Forum Event E-Commerce Free Script Church **Personal** Design Firm Photography Portfolio Web Hosting Web Services Web Software

PERSONAL

The personal site could also be called the ego site since it is hard to assemble one that doesn't feel a bit egocentric. Essentially, these are sites that contain information about an individual. Often they combine a typical portfolio with other information about the owner such as a personal blog or photos. Many personal sites seek to advance the individual's career, but others contain an excess of personal information just for the sake of putting it out there for family, friends or fans to consume.

Regardless of their purpose, personal sites communicate a lot more about an individual than basic portfolio or resume sites. Expanding the site to include other information gives visitors a glimpse into the individual's life. This can be great from a business standpoint

if a potential recruiter views and likes your site. No recruiter would admit to hiring someone for trivial reasons, but connecting with someone's personal interests has powerful sway. If nothing else, the recruiter can see that the individual is a living person beyond his or her wicked CSS skills.

Next Big Leap nicely demonstrates an extended portfolio style that includes extra personal information while maintaining its professionalism. Certainly the site's emphasis is on the individual's job qualifications, but additional information has been included for a more personal look inside the individual's life. Remember that potential employers will likely see the site, so make sure it portrays you in a positive light. Next Big Leap does just that.

http://www.nextbigleap.com

http://www.toddalbertson.com

http://www.mubashariqbal.com

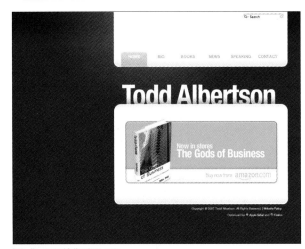

http://www.rommil.com

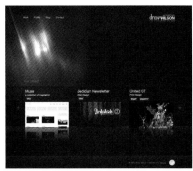

http://www.drewwilson.com

http://www.kadlac.com

http://www.tunnelbound.com

http://chrispederick.com

http://patriciafurtado.com

http://www.jeremyboles.com

SAMPLE COLOR PALETTES

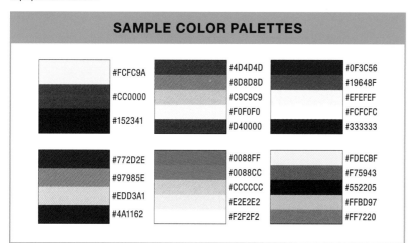

#FCFC9A	
#CC0000	
#152341	

#4D4D4D	#0F3C56
#8D8D8D	#19648F
#C9C9C9	#EFEFEF
#F0F0F0	#FCFCFC
#D40000	#333333

#772D2E	
#97985E	
#EDD3A1	
#4A1162	

#0088FF	#FDECBF
#0088CC	#F75943
#CCCCCC	#552205
#E2E2E2	#FFBD97
#F2F2F2	#FF7220

01

SITES BY TYPE

Blog Forum Event E-Commerce Free Script Church Personal **Design Firm** Photography Portfolio Web Hosting Web Services Web Software

DESIGN FIRM

Deciding how to brand and design for a company that brands and designs for other companies is perhaps one of the most perplexing design problems. There is no right or wrong answer to this problem, as long as the company's message is communicated accurately. That being said, most designers facing this dilemma go for either über-clean or mega-branded style.

In über-clean style, the creative goal is to make the site as simple and minimalist as possible. The company's work samples or studio process should not be overpowered by extraneous graphics, color variations or other design distractions. This method usually results in an abundance of open space, concise navigation, clean crisp type treatments and minimalist color palettes. A great example of this is the Medusateam site. It's crisp, to-the-point, easy to navigate,

and allows the work to shine. The design firm's portfolio takes precedence, and this is a good approach considering the quality of their work.

Mega-branded style establishes a presence through unique brand delivery. The idea is not only to display the studio's capabilities through the work samples and core messaging but also to create a memorable experience that reflects the studio's character with a little "wow factor." Creative firms use this style as their playground to strut and show off a little. The client majority doesn't want or need this type of site, but a mass of bells 'n' whistles accompanied by a highly conceptual brand that is two steps beyond the norm has curb appeal. The goal is to shock and awe its audience. Clients should be blown away, so much so that they can't imagine any limit to the design firm's abilities.

It is surprising how often conservative clients are attracted to creative studios with highly branded, experimental, over-the-top websites. There seems to be a higher level of comfort and confidence that comes from hiring a design firm with an impressive "wow factor." Don't underestimate the power of building a memorable brand site for your studio. It may attract just the right attention.

There are many options when designing for a group of designers. As we all know, we're our own toughest critics. Just keep in mind what you want visitors to take away from the site. Do you want the site to focus on the firm's outstanding work and process? Or do you want to convey a little more about the firm's character by making a lasting impression that is more memorable than the work samples contained within the site?

http://medusateam.com

http://www.ashwebmedia.com

http://www.unleadedsoftware.com

http://www.growstudio.co.uk

http://www.openfieldcreative.com

http://redant.com.au

http://www.silent7.com

http://www.webpuppies.com.sg

http://www.badassembly.com

http://www.monumentstudio.com

SAMPLE COLOR PALETTES

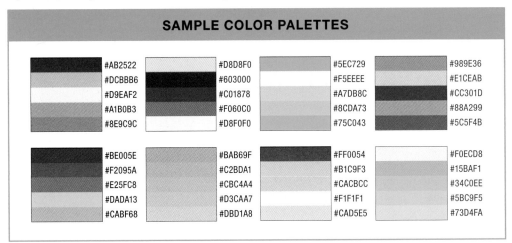

#AB2522		#D8D8F0		#5EC729		#989E36	
#DCBBB6		#603000		#F5EEEE		#E1CEAB	
#D9EAF2		#C01878		#A7DB8C		#CC301D	
#A1B0B3		#F060C0		#8CDA73		#88A299	
#8E9C9C		#D8F0F0		#75C043		#5C5F4B	
#BE005E		#BAB69F		#FF0054		#F0ECD8	
#F2095A		#C2BDA1		#B1C9F3		#15BAF1	
#E25FC8		#CBC4A4		#CACBCC		#34C0EE	
#DADA13		#D3CAA7		#F1F1F1		#5BC9F5	
#CABF68		#DBD1A8		#CAD5E5		#73D4FA	

01
SITES BY TYPE

Blog Forum Event E-Commerce Free Script Church Personal Design Firm **Photography** Portfolio Web Hosting Web Services Web Software

PHOTOGRAPHY

For examples of this site type we will be looking at sites that show photos through a photoblog or a portfolio, not necessarily as photo galleries. In other words, people use photography sites when they want to feature high-quality photos, not snapshots of their family reunion.

What stands out most in these examples is that the presentation style matches the photography style. This correlation is evident in the layouts. Let's start with Georgiew, where a stylish, almost fashion-oriented site design matches just such a photo. There is a connection between the photo and layout in terms of style and color. Another example is the Photoblog of Azin Ashourvan, where we find an ultra-simple layout that just gives us the photo to look at. This minimal design style matches the

minimal style of the photograph. Compare these to the photos found on the Rion site. These photographs have a narrative style that the site design supports. The images flow by, matching the narrative style perfectly.

Some of these design decisions are made accidentally as the designer naturally attempts to match the photographer's style. And many times the photographer is the designer, so the matching style is inevitable. But if you're designing such a site for yourself or for someone else, stop to consider the style of photography and what it has to say about the artist. Then, apply these ideas to the site design in a practical and meaningful way. This goes way beyond matching color. Dig deeper, and you will undoubtedly be inspired.

http://www.georgiew.de

http://blog.azin.se

http://rion.nu

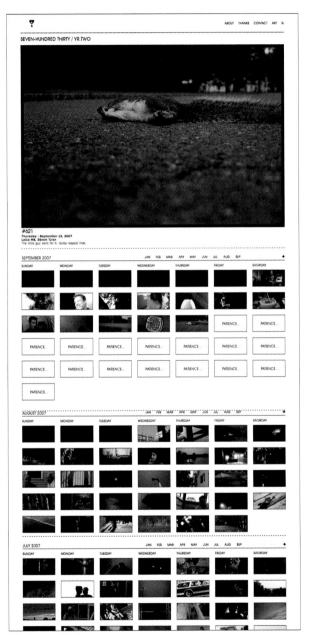

http://www.mattholloway.com

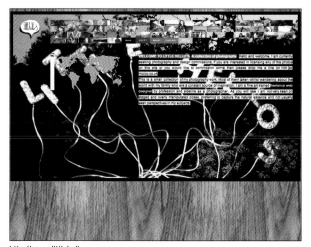

http://www.littlehellos.com

http://www.berdber.com

http://www.nicnichols.com

http://treemeat.com

http://www.peterbyrne.co.uk

http://fotoblog.metaideen.de

http://www.nickbrandt.com

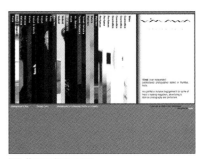

http://www.vimawa.com

http://www.pxldlx.de

http://www.hel-looks.com

SAMPLE COLOR PALETTES

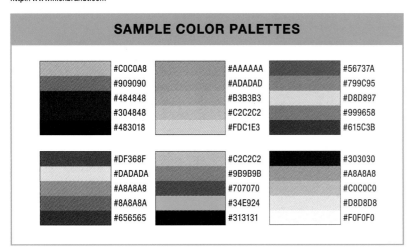

#C0C0A8
#909090
#484848
#304848
#483018

#AAAAAA
#ADADAD
#B3B3B3
#C2C2C2
#FDC1E3

#56737A
#799C95
#D8D897
#999658
#615C3B

#DF368F
#DADADA
#A8A8A8
#8A8A8A
#656565

#C2C2C2
#9B9B9B
#707070
#34E924
#313131

#303030
#A8A8A8
#C0C0C0
#D8D8D8
#F0F0F0

01
SITES BY TYPE

Blog Forum Event E-Commerce Free Script Church Personal Design Firm Photography **Portfolio** Web Hosting Web Services Web Software

PORTFOLIO

Personal portfolio designs are notoriously challenging. Their unlimited potential can be paralyzing. Most designers comment that their current portfolio is about the twentieth variation they made, and typically they only stopped making changes because they gave up. Your first task is to figure out how you need to brand yourself. Too often we long to be something we aren't instead of accepting ourselves with honesty.

Knowing how challenging this task is makes successful portfolio sites all the more enjoyable to see. It seems that the best examples match their site style to the style of their portfolio pieces. When this happens, the unity is powerful. Sure, you can treat your portfolio as a playground, where you can try new things.

But all the same, the site should match your work so people know you understand your niche.

A great example of design and content unity can be seen on Nikki Brion's portfolio site. This designer used a color palette and style that suits her portfolio pieces. Notice how well the color palettes match. The layout adds a great deal of interest to the page as well. Making the content run down the middle does several things. It places focus on the copy, it creates balance and it shows that the artist thinks creatively. This is a fine example of using fresh ideas while retaining the fundamental requirements for a successful portfolio.

Another designer who has established unity between content and pre-

sentation is Steve Leggat. Steve's work appears to have clean and elegant design. His portfolio site plays into this and works well with his samples. While this clean approach lends itself to a simpler site design, he has used a powerful green to create a more memorable experience. After all, you want your portfolio to stand out. A strong color palette can make your site more memorable.

A perfect contrast to the previous design is Ray Hernandez's portfolio. A quick survey of the artist's work reveals a more powerful and bold style. The heavy black-and-white design of the site provides consistency. Interestingly, the color palette keeps the page design from conflicting with the heavier images in this portfolio.

http://nb.bottledsky.com

http://www.stoodio.com

http://steveleggat.com

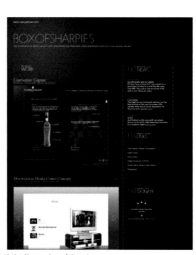

http://www.boxofsharpies.com

http://www.gearboxmedia.net

http://www.bnweiss.com

http://www.michaelnixdesign.com/

http://pixelimplosion.com

http://www.tonick.cz

http://www.dache.ch

http://www.albertocerriteno.com

http://www.dominikwroblewski.com

http://jonkeegan.com

http://www.natepercell.com/portfolio

SAMPLE COLOR PALETTES

	#FFFFFF		#673319		#600000		#6B0000
	#B1DDD4		#F1AA3D		#901818		#F6CC95
	#602310		#EA7431		#A81818		#8D876B
	#DDE295		#FFF96E		#90C048		#F6C229
	#000000		#B1291D		#487818		#D7C374
	#6F3481		#543A24		#6A5443		#EAB289
	#000000		#2D1B0B		#7CA0CC		#D9EA89
	#FFFFFF		#7EC47E		#D84F4F		#E9E9E9
	#F5F5F5		#D9E6CB		#F7F6F5		#BBBBBB
	#D4D4D4		#EDEDDA		#FFFFFF		#6D6D6D

01
SITES BY TYPE

Blog Forum Event E-Commerce Free Script Church Personal Design Firm Photography Portfolio **Web Hosting** Web Services Web Software

WEB HOSTING

The sites that represent web hosting companies face the same potential problems that plague other types of sites, so they can be great sources of inspiration when they are designed and implemented well. After all, creating a beautiful design is only half the problem; making the design a reality requires effective implementation.

The first problem these sites face is info glut. There is just so much information, like price points, storage space, bandwidth, server features and control panels, to be communicated to potential clients. It is tempting to try to emphasize everything in a bloated list like this, but if you try to emphasize everything, you succeed at emphasizing nothing.

HostedFX demonstrates one of the cleanest solutions to this problem. The homepage provides all the needed information and even includes some small details for potential clients, but it still adheres to the design principle of hierarchy. By prioritizing the displayed content, the site doesn't obscure the real goal, which is to get clients to sign up. Amid all this information the "get started" and "order now" buttons still manage to stand out. This heavy dose of content is presented in a manageable way that is easily consumable.

The second problem that many web hosting firms face is an overly technical mindset. As a consumer, I personally appreciate when web-hosting services focus on technology over design. However, a well-designed site helps sell their products to design-conscious people, who represent the majority of the population. The second step in great design is great implementation, and the EarnersHost site has offers an impressive example of this. Not only do they have a wonderful design, but they also managed to implement it beautifully. Often, a design falls apart when faced with reality, and it ends up looking as though essential elements were stuffed into it. The EarnersHost design, on the other hand, seems to have been well planned. The result is a polished site that puts this company a step above other web hosting options.

http://www.hostedfx.com

http://www.earnershost.com

http://www.enginehosting.com

http://www.abysslevel.net

http://www.doreo.com

http://www.wiredtree.com

http://www.intelero.com

http://www.sherweb.com

http://blogs-about.com

http://www.mosso.com

http://tribolis.com

http://www.site5.com

http://www.idebagus.com

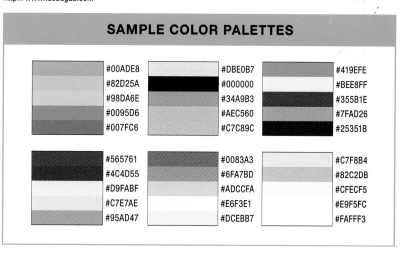

SAMPLE COLOR PALETTES

#00ADE8	#DBE0B7	#419EFE
#82D25A	#000000	#BEE8FF
#98DA6E	#34A9B3	#355B1E
#0095D6	#AEC560	#7FAD26
#007FC6	#C7C89C	#25351B
#565761	#0083A3	#C7F8B4
#4C4D55	#6FA7BD	#82C2DB
#D9FABF	#ADCCFA	#CFECF5
#C7E7AE	#E6F3E1	#E9F5FC
#95AD47	#DCEBB7	#FAFFF3

01

SITES BY TYPE

Blog Forum Event E-Commerce Free Script Church Personal Design Firm Photography Portfolio Web Hosting Web Services Web Software

WEB SERVICES

Web services are any website that offers a mini application. These applications are usually very focused and play a supportive role; they include things like form processors and builders or file storage services. Web services sites are appealing to web developers and almost anybody working over the Internet.

Web services can be a tough sell. The first issue I have with them is trying to figure out what the heck they do, or if I even need them. There is nothing more infuriating than being on the hunt for a specific application and landing on sites that don't clearly explain what their product actually does. These sample sites have avoided this trap entirely. In fact, even a small thumbnail of the site conveys its purpose. This is saying a lot; the sites have succeeded at making their services as clear as possible.

This same principle could be applied to nearly any type of site. Blogs come to mind first. I find it annoying to land on a blog and not have a clue what the topic or purpose of it is. Is it personal? Professional? What is the topic? This lack of communication can suck the life and momentum right out of a product.

One thing all these samples share is a big, bold, clear statement about what the product is. They don't rely on a name, logo or screenshot to do the speaking. Instead, they lay it out there as plainly as possible. It may seem like they are stating the obvious, but a first-time visitor will find the statement very helpful. "Easily Access and Share Files," "Dead-Simple File Sharing," and "Web Forms and Surveys in Just Minutes" are all examples of the blunt but enlightening descriptions on sites in this category.

http://www.majikwidget.com

http://box.net

http://wufoo.com

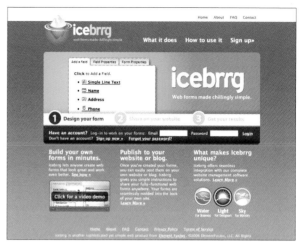

http://www.icebrrg.com

http://www.listphile.com

http://www.pingdom.com

041

http://www.boxcloud.com

http://keepm.com

http://www.aiderss.com

http://www.formsite.com

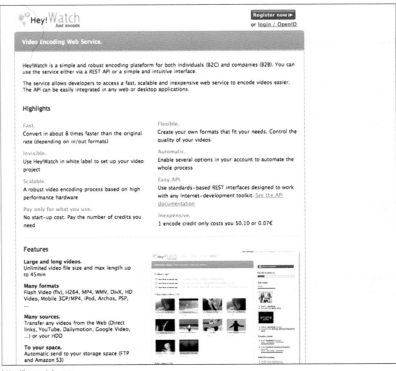

Video Encoding Web Service.

Hey!Watch is a simple and robust encoding plateform for both individuals (B2C) and companies (B2B). You can use the service either via a REST API or a simple and intuitive interface.

The service allows developers to access a fast, scalable and inexpensive web service to encode videos easier. The API can be easily integrated in any web or desktop applications.

Highlights

Fast.
Convert in about 8 times faster than the original rate (depending on in/out formats)

Invisible.
Use Hey!Watch in white label to set up your video project

Scalable.
A robust video encoding process based on high performance hardware

Pay only for what you use.
No start-up cost. Pay the number of credits you need

Flexible.
Create your own formats that fit your needs. Control the quality of your videos

Automatic.
Enable several options in your account to automate the whole process

Easy API.
Use standards-based REST interfaces designed to work with any Internet-development toolkit. See the API documentation

Inexpensive.
1 encode credit only costs you $0.10 or 0.07€

Features

Large and long videos.
Unlimited video file size and max length up to 45min

Many formats.
Flash Video (flv), H264, MP4, WMV, DivX, HD Video, Mobile 3GP/MP4, iPod, Archos, PSP, ...

Many sources.
Transfer any videos from the Web (Direct links, YouTube, Dailymotion, Google Video, ...) or your HDD

To your space.
Automatic send to your storage space (FTP and Amazon S3)

http://heywatch.com

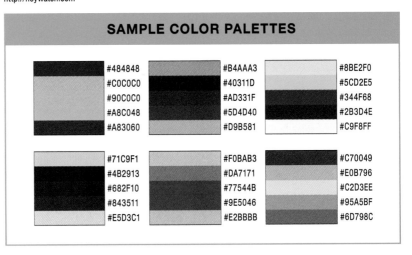

SAMPLE COLOR PALETTES

#484848		#B4AAA3		#8BE2F0
#C0C0C0		#40311D		#5CD2E5
#90C0C0		#AD331F		#344F68
#A8C048		#5D4D40		#2B3D4E
#A83060		#D9B581		#C9F8FF

#71C9F1		#F0BAB3		#C70049
#4B2913		#DA7171		#E0B796
#682F10		#77544B		#C2D3EE
#843511		#9E5046		#95A5BF
#E5D3C1		#E2BBBB		#6D798C

01
SITES BY TYPE

Blog Forum Event E-Commerce Free Script Church Personal Design Firm Photography Portfolio Web Hosting Web Services **Web Software**

WEB SOFTWARE

Web software sites are closely related to—and in some ways indistinguishable from—web services sites. Web software sites are websites offering applications that would otherwise be a stand-alone package for installation on a machine. Web services sites, on the other hand, offer features that are not on a PC, and are disconnected from the web (think bookmaking, file sharing, etc.).

One thing I noticed right away about these applications is that many of them use blue and green color palettes. This is an interesting coincidence that probably stems from the fact that web software is used by a broad audience. For example, there is a huge variety of people who need to track billable time.

Consequently, the design of a site that offers such an application must be universally appealing. Tick is just such site. Its blue-and-green color palette is safe and works wonderfully to create a warm and welcoming environment, not to mention the fact that it gives the software an easy-to-use feel.

As a site representing a product, Campaign Monitor has a remarkable design feature. Everything is a shade of blue, except for the single most important element on the page. The "create a free account" button stands out because it is yellow. The yellow button manages to fit into the design without looking out of place, yet it is the major focal point in the design. Clearly, the

designers knew what action point they wanted to emphasize most. Another key element of the design is the clear explanation of what the product does. This statement appears in the banner of the page, and its impact is undeniable.

Another piece of web software that is presented in an appropriate package appears on the Big Cartel site. The site offers e-commerce software geared toward individuals and small businesses that want to sell merchandise over the Internet. This site design targets a hip crowd that is interested in aesthetics. The fancy edge along the top, the semi-distressed background and a trendy color palette all combine to create an appealing design.

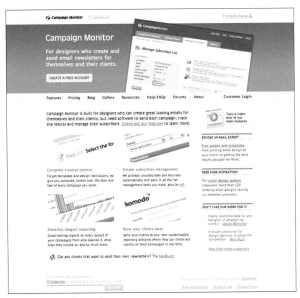

http://www.campaignmonitor.com

http://www.tickspot.com

http://www.bigcartel.com

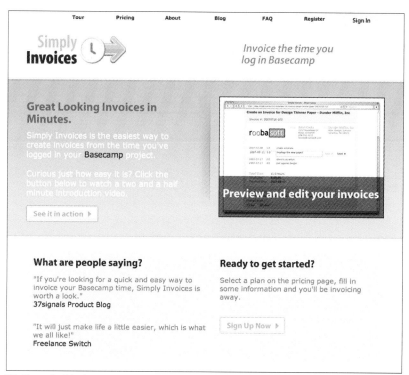

http://www.simplyinvoices.com

http://www.slimtimer.com

http://www.feelbreeze.com

http://www.mochibot.com

http://www.lessaccounting.com

http://www.relenta.com

http://crazyegg.com

http://www.cogmap.com

http://squirl.info

http://pbwiki.com

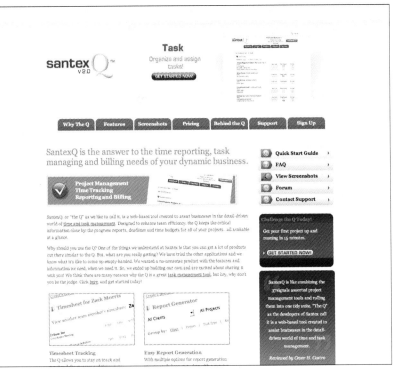

http://www.santexq.com

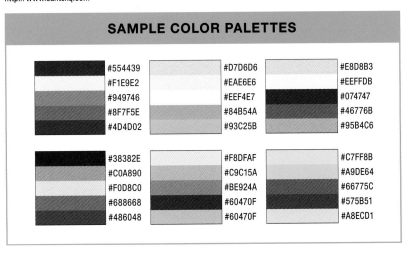

SAMPLE COLOR PALETTES

#554439	#D7D6D6	#E8D8B3
#F1E9E2	#EAE6E6	#EEFFDB
#949746	#EEF4E7	#074747
#8F7F5E	#84B54A	#46776B
#4D4D02	#93C25B	#95B4C6
#38382E	#F8DFAF	#C7FF8B
#C0A890	#C9C15A	#A9DE64
#F0D8C0	#BE924A	#66775C
#688668	#60470F	#575B51
#486048	#60470F	#A8ECD1

046

02

SITES BY DESIGN STYLE

Design styles tend to represent larger movements and patterns in the design world. Styles don't typically have specific elements associated with them, but rather are marked by their visuals. These could be defined as overall theories in the approach to design. Minimalism is a prime example of how a particular design can drive what the artist produces. This style defines how a site will look and feel, but it doesn't dictate any specific imagery. Other styles, such as retro, collage, distressed and sketchy, are more specific, with obvious patterns and clear visual results. Deciding on a style should by no means be arbitrary. The style in which a site is presented is of the utmost importance and should be carefully planned so as to contribute to the overall brand and message of a site.

02

SITES BY DESIGN STYLE

Retro Minimalist Super-Clean Distressed Three-Dimensional Sketchy Collage Illustrated Photographic Giant Type Let the Art Speak

RETRO

Revised versions of past styles are common and popular. Retro style is found in advertising, CD design, fashion and, of course, web design. It can be employed for a variety of reasons. Sometimes this style is driven by the content of the site, and other times it is chosen for its conceptual association with the past.

There are three key elements that create a retro feel when combined. To use this style successfully, consider how all three of these elements work together to make a complete theme.

The color palette. An appropriate color palette is fundamental to establishing a retro style. The period you are shooting for will ultimately determine the set of colors you choose. Earth tones are common on retro sites. They make things appear aged even though they are not associated with a specific time period.

Rockbeatspaper is a great example of how color can create a retro feel. The palette is reminiscent of the 1970s. The color palette single-handedly achieves the site's retro style, demonstrating the power that color choice has over style.

Old photography or illustration. In nearly all the sites, photography or illustration is the primary element that sets the atmosphere. Without the imagery, most of these sites would fail at pulling viewers into a different era. For example, the TargetScope website has an illustration of a pinup model. This is easily understood as a reference to the 1940s. That, combined with the military theme, clearly plants us in the midst of World War II. Imagine the layout without the model and you will quickly see how important it is. The other primary image is the background. The paper texture ages the site and completes the whole retro package.

Retro typefaces. Typefaces can either complete or destroy a design. Finding appropriate retro typefaces can be difficult. Some styles fit specific eras, like the flowing bubbly letters of the 1960s and 1970s. Many fonts fit certain time periods more generically (typewriter fonts, for example).

Consider the CakePHP website. The color palette lends itself to the 1950s, as do the rounded, angular shapes. But it is the type treatment of the title and buttons that reminds us most of that time period. Don't skimp when it comes to selecting typefaces. It is easy to abuse decorative fonts, but when applied with skill, they can really enhance the design of a site. On many of the samples, a more decorative, period-appropriate typeface has been used for the main title of the site, while more subtle fonts have been selected for the supporting copy.

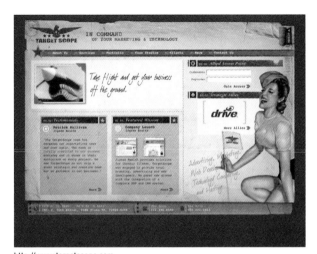

http://www.targetscope.com

http://www.cakephp.org

http://rockbeatspaper.net

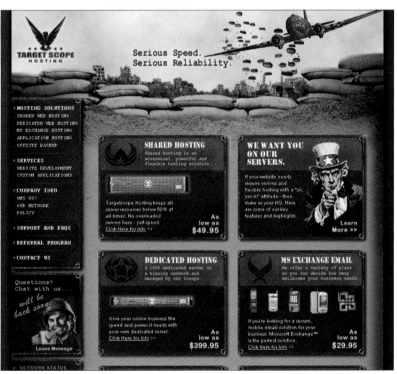

http://www.targetscopehosting.com

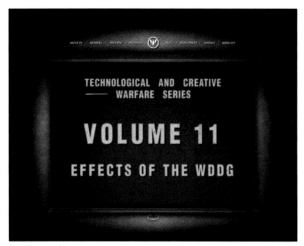

http://www.wddg.com

http://www.detektiv-nali.de

http://www.bombippy.com

http://www.mondomochales.com

http://www.fontdiner.com

http://www.maniacmonkeymedia.com

http://www.puchlerz.com

http://dollardreadful.com

SAMPLE COLOR PALETTES

#6E5300	#070604	#000000	#44CCA5	#907830
#B0AD08	#69604B	#F01848	#E26D29	#F0D860
#FFA400	#EECF54	#F07800	#F3EABF	#A86018
#A1D8D9	#DDD8CE	#C00030	#C6F169	#909048
#D15100	#283D6B	#F0A800	#7DDAAA	#907830

#F3F2E9	#EBEBEB	#481800	#D8C090	#904830
#7EB6B3	#DDD95E	#F07800	#F0F0A5	#A8C030
#682525	#F06F0A	#48A8C0	#C00003	#F0F090
#E9E9A1	#470F04	#483018	#786047	#D87830
#313131	#AD5416	#A8D848	#303032	#F0A8C0

02

SITES BY DESIGN STYLE

Retro **Minimalist** Super-Clean Distressed Three-Dimensional Sketchy Collage Illustrated Photographic Giant Type Let the Art Speak

MINIMALIST

Minimalist style reduces presentation to its most basic elements; gone are most flourishes and aesthetic elements. It is unusual to come across purely minimal design and even more unusual to find great examples of it. However, it is rather easy to find sites that adhere to the majority of minimalist principles with just enough extra ornament to make them stunning examples of the style.

Minimalism is understated. Most people don't understand the beauty of minimal design. To most it just looks simple, and at the same time, effective.

It is often assumed that a minimalist design is easy to create. On the contrary, designing with the bare essentials is far more difficult than it looks.

One of the benefits of minimal design is that it reduces clutter. This allows the content to stand out and produces a design that is very easy to consume. This is great for users with short attention spans. On the other hand, minimalist style tends to have less flare, which means the content must stand strongly on its own to grab the visitors' attention.

http://www.tbgd.co.uk

http://www.endcommunications.com

http://www.studiorobot.com.au

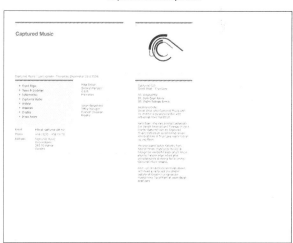

http://microformatique.com

http://minifolio.binaryvein.com

http://www.captured.nu

http://www.filosof.biz

http://androo.com

http://www.openedhand.com

http://www.terracestudios.co.uk

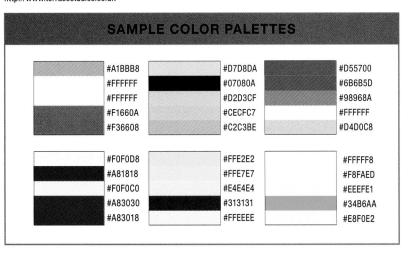

SAMPLE COLOR PALETTES

#A1BBB8	#D7D8DA
#FFFFFF	#07080A
#FFFFFF	#D2D3CF
#F1660A	#CECFC7
#F36608	#C2C3BE

#D55700	
#6B6B5D	
#98968A	
#FFFFFF	
#D4D0C8	

#F0F0D8	#FFE2E2
#A81818	#FFE7E7
#F0F0C0	#E4E4E4
#A83030	#313131
#A83018	#FFEEEE

#FFFFF8
#F8FAED
#EEEEFE1
#34B6AA
#E8F0E2

02
SITES BY DESIGN STYLE

Retro   Minimalist   **Super-Clean**   Distressed   Three-Dimensional   Sketchy   Collage   Illustrated   Photographic   Giant Type   Let the Art Speak

SUPER-CLEAN

This category represents the combination of several design principles. The heart of super-clean style is that, visually speaking, these designs are super-clean. (How about that for a circular reference?) These could be considered ideal or ultimate designs. The example sites in this category are uncluttered, have plenty of breathing room, have a clear hierarchy, and are balanced and easy to consume.

The perfect example of super-clean style is the Spacemaker site. The design is clean and elegant, the entire page is balanced, and elements are pleasingly distributed. The hierarchy of the page is carefully controlled through the use of scale, contrast and color, and space is used wisely, allowing plenty of breathing room around elements to avoid overcrowding. All these factors combine to make the site very easy to consume.

An example with less content is the Pixelpanic site, which maintains its super-clean style with excellent color choice and plenty of breathing room for a light and comfortable page. Again, all of the elements have been generously spaced to avoid a cluttered feel. The site is so simple, yet so complex.

Finally, take a look at the arc90 site, where we find yet another example of super-clean style. The extreme attention to hierarchy is what makes this site so easy to consume. Notice how the content blurbs don't compete for dominance with the titles and headings, yet they are reasonably sized and legible.

http://www.spacemakerwardrobes.com.au

http://pixelpanic.be

http://lab.arc90.com

http://www.coreaudiovisual.com

http://www.clandrei.de

http://www.period-three.com

http://www.whalesalad.com

http://www.mediact.nl

http://www.protolize.org

http://simplebits.com

http://new-bamboo.co.uk

http://www.achtentachtig.com

http://www.joshclarkportfolio.com

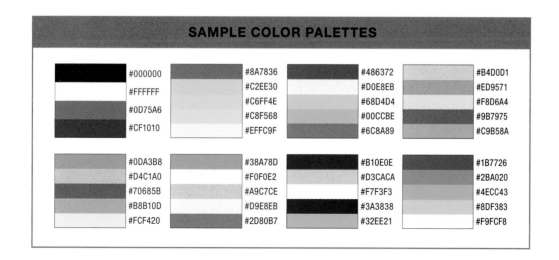

SAMPLE COLOR PALETTES

#000000		#8A7836		#486372		#B4D0D1	
#FFFFFF		#C2EE30		#D0E8EB		#ED9571	
#0D75A6		#C6FF4E		#68D4D4		#F8D6A4	
#CF1010		#C8F568		#00CCBE		#9B7975	
		#EFFC9F		#6C8A89		#C9B58A	

#0DA3B8		#38A78D		#B10E0E		#1B7726	
#D4C1A0		#F0F0E2		#D3CACA		#2BA020	
#70685B		#A9C7CE		#F7F3F3		#4ECC43	
#B8B10D		#D9E8EB		#3A3838		#8DF383	
#FCF420		#2D80B7		#32EE21		#F9FCF8	

02
SITES BY DESIGN STYLE

Retro · Minimalist · Super-Clean · **Distressed** · Three-Dimensional · Sketchy · Collage · Illustrated · Photographic · Giant Type · Let the Art Speak

DISTRESSED

The usage of distressed elements in design is nothing new, and perhaps the golden age of textured web design has passed. All this really means is that gratuitous and meaningless texture on websites is no longer accepted. Current sites use texture for a deliberate purpose, meaning and quality. As with any trend, this one has passed the stage of overuse and evolved into a refined approach to solving specific design problems. Like many other elements, the most common reason to employ distressed elements is to create an atmosphere or mood on a site.

Many sites use texture simply to break up the computer-generated feel of straight lines, solid colors and perfect gradients. The Urban International site is a prime example of this. In this case the distressed background breaks up the perfect vector shapes and gives the site a stylized feel. The texture adds richness to the design that would otherwise not exist.

Perhaps the strongest use of texture is in the effort to express creativity. Sites like Designs by Patima aptly demonstrate this approach. As a site representing a designer and artist, Designs by Patima suits the personal portfolio format very well.

Some sites, like Sourhaze, apply the style in an extreme fashion. Others, such as the 9th Wave site, use it in more subtle ways. Clearly, the texture on these two sites serves different purposes. The Sourhaze design has a far grittier feel, which matches the industrial, gritty style of the featured music. The 9th Wave site has a more conservative style and represents a firm that is probably less radical than Sourhaze, so the more restrained texture suits this site well. It provides a bit of style without getting too grungy.

It would be putting it mildly to say that texture has been abused. Despite this, it is still a powerful and expressive tool designers can employ to solve problems and communicate messages effectively. Just as with any other design element, you must first decide if it reinforces your message. If the theme fits, run with it. Sites that use this element well can be quite gorgeous.

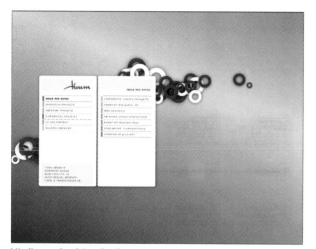

http://www.urban-international.com

http://www.9thwave.co.uk

http://www.sourhaze.com/v7

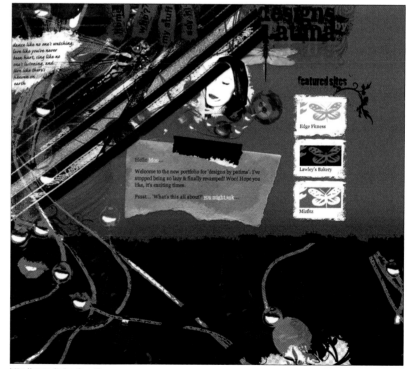

http://www.designsbypatima.com

http://www.beyondjazz.net

http://www.imotion-media.nl/eng

http://www.satsu.co.uk

http://www.akanai.com

http://www.jasonsantamaria.com

http://www.kutztown.edu/acad/commdes

http://www.bitflydesign.com

http://strzibny.name/strzibny

http://www.triplux.com

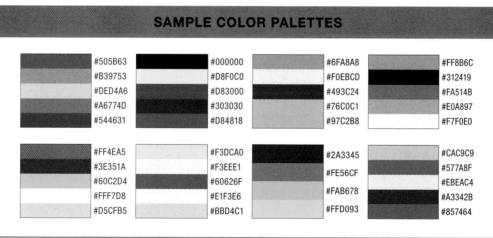

SAMPLE COLOR PALETTES

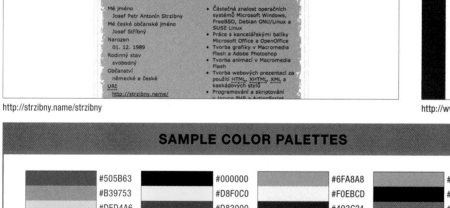

#505B63
#B39753
#DED4A6
#A6774D
#544631

#000000
#D8F0C0
#D83000
#303030
#D84818

#6FA8A8
#F0EBCD
#493C24
#76C0C1
#97C2B8

#FF8B6C
#312419
#FA514B
#E0A897
#F7F0E0

#FF4EA5
#3E351A
#60C2D4
#FFF7D8
#D5CFB5

#F3DCA0
#F3EEE1
#60626F
#E1F3E6
#BBD4C1

#2A3345
#FE56CF
#FAB678
#FFD093

#CAC9C9
#577A8F
#EBEAC4
#A3342B
#857464

02
SITES BY DESIGN STYLE

Retro Minimalist Super-Clean Distressed **Three-Dimensional** Sketchy Collage Illustrated Photographic Giant Type Let the Art Speak

THREE-DIMENSIONAL

The Internet tends to be flat and static, which makes it quite refreshing to run across a site with some breathing space. Adding a three-dimensional feel to aspects of a design is a great way to enhance the overall visual interest and set the page apart. This approach tends to give a site a unique and spacious feel that is somehow both comforting and visually interesting.

Typically when the term "three-dimensional" comes up, most people run for the hills, assuming it is a difficult path to head down. Visions of wire frames and insanely complex applications scare the thought right out of their heads. This doesn't have to be the case, however. In fact, many of the samples provided here create the illusion of depth with simple techniques and visual tricks.

The most commonly used trick is overlapping elements. This works particularly well when one of the elements is an image of a physical object. By overlapping the image with the page design, a sense of depth is established. Our mind is tricked into believing the space is there because we know the object is not flat. And if the object is not flat, it simply must exist in that space.

The key is to select an image that shows the viewer something that is known to occupy space. Use a person, a computer, a bucket of paint or an apple—anything our mind can't avoid putting in a physical space. The object must also be cut out around its edges so it appears to be standing in the space. If it is presented as a photograph with a white border, the illusion will fail miserably unless you're intentionally making it look like a photo

that exists in a three-dimensional space. Learning how to mask images in Adobe Photoshop is your best bet for success.

Another simple technique is the use of shadows. A shadow on nearly anything makes it appear to stand up, thereby creating the illusion of space. This works particularly well when the shadow appears to descend away from the object.

A wonderful example of this can be found on the portfolio site of Colin McKinney. The illusion of depth in this design couldn't be more effective. Our mind knows that the figure must occupy space, so the background is naturally pushed away from us. This also draws the paper in his hand toward us, further emphasizing the main navigation and giving it visual priority on the page. Thus this simple implementation has a very practical purpose.

http://www.colinmckinney.co.uk

http://www.peepshow.org.uk

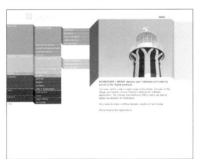

http://schroeder-wendt.com

http://www.softgray.com

http://www.thomasmarban.com

http://www.noodlebox.be

http://www.gonzales.be

http://www.cubedesigners.com

02
SITES BY DESIGN STYLE

Retro Minimalist Super-Clean Distressed Three-Dimensional **Sketchy** Collage Illustrated Photographic Giant Type Let the Art Speak

SKETCHY

Anyone who has been through art school—drawing classes in particular—can appreciate the sketchy elements included in this category. The sketchy style allows artists to put these skills to use, as we will see demonstrated in the following sites. Formally trained artists go to great lengths to learn controlled drawing and painting, so it is perhaps this familiarity that attracts them to sketchy style.

To accomplish this style, elements are drawn by hand and scanned into the computer. These images are then combined with more typical computer-generated design elements. It is also common to add elements with grit and texture, like stained and torn paper, scanned tape, scratchy textures and anything else to further relate the design to tangible, handmade elements. (This can eventually lead to collage style.)

This technique can produce fantastic results. The connotations are clear, and it works tremendously well to communicate creativity and an artistic touch. Sketchy style is a smart choice for artists or for sites related to creativity. This style suits creative agencies perfectly. The Kinetic Singapore site is a great example of this. This creative agency site features an animation that is based on sketchy style. While watching it, viewers can literally see the artist's hand in it. In this way the site achieves its goals of connecting viewers with the agency's creative side and convincing clients of the agency's ability to solve visual problems.

The sketchy style can quickly lead to a collage design with a do-it-yourself feel. The Cambrian House site is an example of this. The real beauty of this example is how the sketchy style supports the purpose of the site, which is to help people turn their ideas into reality. The sketchy style makes me think of someone scribbling an idea down on a napkin. It feels fresh and instantaneous—just like a great idea.

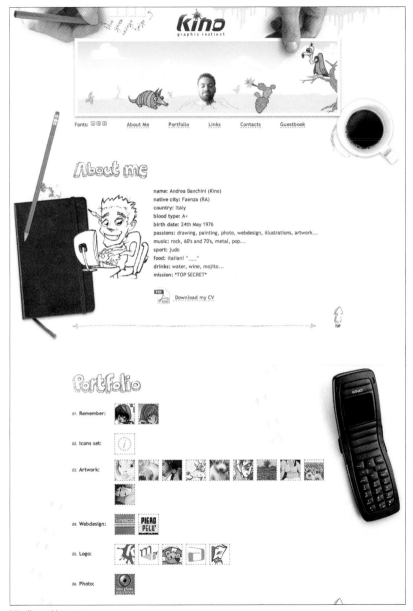

http://www.kinoz.com

http://www.kinetic.com.sg

http://www.cambrianhouse.com

http://www.thebutchershop.com.au

065

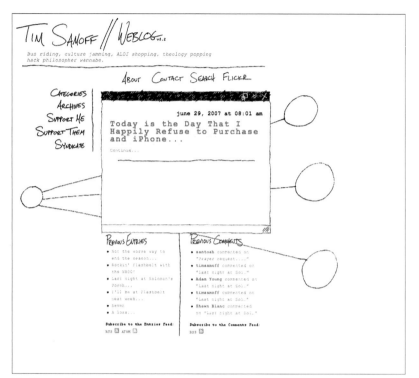

http://tim.samoff.com

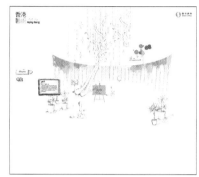

http://www.artinhk.com

http://www.midwestisbest.com

http://smallfriescookbook.com

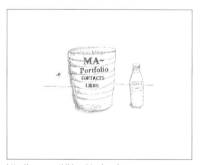

http://www.mathildeaubier.free.fr

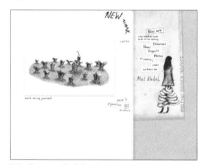

http://www.melkadel.com

02
SITES BY DESIGN STYLE

Retro Minimalist Super-Clean Distressed Three-Dimensional Sketchy **Collage** Illustrated Photographic Giant Type Let the Art Speak

COLLAGE

The collage as a style for web design presents many interesting problems and opportunities. Foremost of the problems is how to translate a collage-based design into an actual web page. The graphical complexity of such designs tends to lead to problems. However, the same basic methods apply and can be easier than expected to implement.

The first option is to use large images, image maps and cascading style sheets (CSS). CSS-based sites are all the rage these days, and rightfully so. It has essentially become the "proper" way to build a site. Upon initial inspection, a collage-based design may seem difficult to translate into CSS. There are many CSS methods available that make it easier than expected, though. The best thing about using CSS instead of tables is that you don't have to slice the images up as much. With tables you have to chop them into tons of little pieces, but with CSS you can use larger background images and place containers of text over them.

The second key method is to use Flash as a medium of implementation. Flash offers the most flexibility to the collage-based site. It allows you to incorporate animation, and the latest version of Flash enables layer blending modes that can be of great use. People of all experience levels can do Flash-based sites. High-end users will find unlimited power in them, and new users will find the ability to build a site quickly without having to jump many technical hurdles. Perhaps the best feature of Flash is its lack of browser-related problems. The pixel-perfect nature of collage-based sites can lead to heavy cross-browser-testing.

http://www.rmusic.co.uk

http://www.timeforcake.com

http://www.fracture.co.nz

http://44suburbia.org

http://www.yozzan.com

http://d3zin3.net

http://stolendesign.net

http://www.atelierdetour.ch

http://www.tylergaw.com

SAMPLE COLOR PALETTES

#0078A8	#90D8D8	#990003
#304860	#78C0A8	#FFAFA3
#A89078	#D8D818	#EA444E
#780048	#F0D818	#630E13
#C03078	#D80018	#980000

#303048	#251B11	#FFCF55
#484860	#5D4A39	#FAAD25
#D8D860	#372B1F	#FC7A17
#C0C030	#99846F	#9ECFC5
#D8C030	#7E6956	#B84A0C

02
SITES BY DESIGN STYLE

Retro Minimalist Super-Clean Distressed Three-Dimensional Sketchy Collage **Illustrated** Photographic Giant Type Let the Art Speak

ILLUSTRATED

Illustration is not nearly as common in web design as one might expect. In print design, photography and illustration are relied upon heavily. The web, however, seems to focus more on photography, most likely because of the cheap and easy-to-use nature of photography. This is not to say that photography is truly easy, but it is far easier than illustration for the average person to master.

Many of the sites displayed here would be entirely forgettable if they had not included an illustration. Others are completely developed around the illustration with the entire design stemming from it. This is a fun set of sites to browse through because each site has a distinct feel, and the illustrations set the mood. Illustrations don't have to be bubbly or light. Like photography, they can create any atmosphere one might need.

Illustration is a harder and more expensive route, but using illustrations in your web design is a recipe for uniqueness. How lame would the Intuitive Designs site be if they had used a stock photo of a chef? Instead, they have a wonderful illustration that fits the design and message of the site. And even better, the site stands out.

In a medium that is flooded with thousands of options, it is critical for a site to stand out. One that is not easily forgotten is the site for the creative agency Web.Burza. Never underestimate the ability of a design agency to showcase its talent through its own site. Their homepage alone sells them, long before you reach their portfolio. Brilliant use of illustration has truly created a unique atmosphere for this site.

A great example of how an illustration can steer the entire design of a site

is the personal portfolio site of Brent Ayers. Instead of slapping an illustration into the banner and then designing the rest with disregard, the designer has carefully crafted the entire site to work with the illustration. Or, was it done the other way around? That's the beauty of doing this well—no one can tell which came first. The point is to see the whole picture; often this is where photography fails. Sometimes photography is slapped in without regard for the design as a whole. The cost and effort required for illustration safeguard against this.

In many instances where photography could be forced to do the job, it is best not to settle. Such is the case with the Octonauts site. Here the site is a big success because of its wise illustration choice. It is easy to see how photography could have been used, but not nearly as effectively.

http://www.intuitivedesigns.net

http://web.burza.hr

http://www.octonauts.com

http://www.brentayers.com

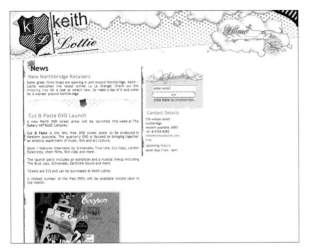

http://www.keithandlottie.com

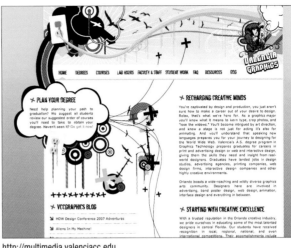

http://multimedia.valenciacc.edu

http://www.areeba.com.au

http://www.smallandround.com

http://www.leuyenpham.com

http://www.aquaboogie.net

http://deborahcavenaugh.com

http://www.philinehartert.com

02
SITES BY DESIGN STYLE

Retro Minimalist Super-Clean Distressed Three-Dimensional Sketchy Collage Illustrated **Photographic** Giant Type Let the Art Speak

PHOTOGRAPHIC

Using photographic backgrounds sounds like a terrible 1995 sort of idea ... until you see sites that use them well. Every one of these sites feels fresh and new, with the photographs lending an element that is far more organic than the typical web stuff.

For an example of good literal use of this element, take a look at the Deco-mart site. This is an extremely small site with only two pages. What makes this simple little business-card-style site great is that viewers can pretty well guess the site's purpose within two seconds of seeing it. The photo is beautiful and conveys a message efficiently. Too often these sorts of photographs are contained to small side shots or typical banners. What a delight it is to find a creative use such as this. And in this case, the photograph saves the site from being dull.

The 2Advanced Studios site puts the background image to a slightly different use. The space-age image doesn't explain what the company does, but once we realize it is a creative agency the point becomes clear. This is a very graphic and creative bunch of people. The purpose of the illustration is to create an atmosphere that says something about the company. Sure, this blurs the line between photography and illustration, but the image is still used as a massive, dominant background.

The portfolio site of Javier Alvear Ruiz-Rivas uses the photographic background purely for aesthetic purposes. However, this use is not detrimental to the site. In fact, countless elements are used on the web for the sake of beauty, and this simple portfolio site would be rather bleak without its decorative image. This site is a prime example of how the

photograph should match the site and the color scheme.

Another important thing to note when using this style is that a complex background image forces the foreground to be more restrained. This must be done to avoid an unpleasantly busy page, but it is a wonderful side effect because it makes things easier to flesh out. The Design and Image Communications site demonstrates this balance perfectly. The content appears on top of the photograph and is designed in such a way that it is readable and balanced. The containers for the content are minimal but finely crafted.

Do not underestimate the power of this element. But remember that with great power comes great responsibility. This style can be bold, powerful and meaningful, but it can also be absolutely horrible when implemented poorly.

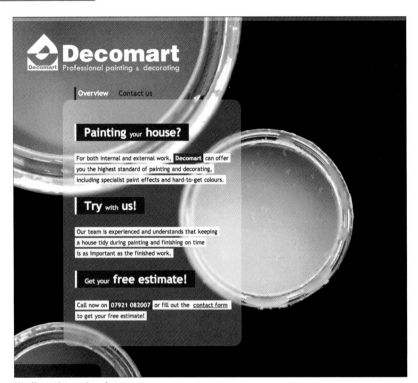

http://www.decomart.co.uk

http://www.2advanced.com

http://www.analogue.ca

http://www.evoland.es

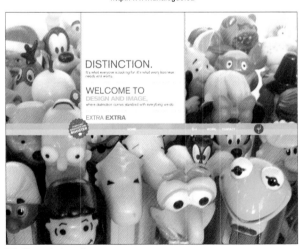

http://www.designandimage.com

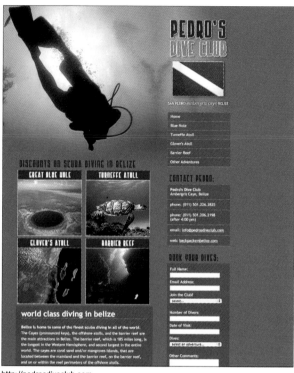

http://pedrosdiveclub.com

http://www.superieur-graphique.com

http://www.herbatonica.com

http://www.swivelheaddesign.com

http://www.secondstory.com

02

SITES BY DESIGN STYLE

Retro   Minimalist   Super-Clean   Distressed   Three-Dimensional   Sketchy   Collage   Illustrated   Photographic   **Giant Type**   Let the Art Speak

GIANT TYPE

The use of giant typography on the web is not only an attractive style, but it is also practical and addresses key design issues. First, and perhaps most obviously, it absolutely reeks of hierarchy, which is a basic design principle. One of the key methods for establishing hierarchy in a design is through scale, and these sites have certainly taken this approach to an extreme. If you are asking yourself why this is important, remember that enabling users to consume a chunk of content (in any medium) easily is imperative. If users look at something huge and daunting with no sense of hierarchy, and thus, no place to start, they will be tempted to give up.

Hierarchy effortlessly provides consumers the information they are after. I can't count the number of times I have found an online tutorial for coding something and have used the page's hierarchy to skip the explanation and go straight to the solution!

Secondly, and very much related to the first point, giant type effectively beats the user over the head with a message. The Finch site is a great example of this. Before visitors get to the meat of the site, they are presented with a minimized homepage and a bold message that leaves no doubt about what the company does. This is so refreshing considering the number of confusing sites for design shops that don't make their service obviously known. The Finch site clears the air and lays it out there; the large type ensures that the visitor at least gets this fundamental message, not to mention that the bold type is absolutely beautiful and shows that they get good typographic design. This bold statement sums up the firm in every way.

Large type lets the designer employ the natural beauty of typefaces and provides a megaphone with which to speak. This jumbo-sized type will become the focus of the page if you make use of the style, so be sure to say something important!

http://www.getfinch.com

http://www.jeffreydocherty.com

http://www.plainsimple.dk

http://www.citrus7.com.br

http://www.organicgrid.com

http://www.bureausla.nl

http://www.martinkonrad.com.au

http://blogsolid.com

http://www.darrenalawi.com

02

SITES BY DESIGN STYLE

Retro Minimalist Super-Clean Distressed Three-Dimensional Sketchy Collage Illustrated Photographic Giant Type **Let the Art Speak**

LET THE ART SPEAK

Sometimes your best bet is to just put it all out there. Lay it out, and let the world see you for what you are. This is exactly what the sites in this category have done. The design approach that all of these websites share is a body of outstanding and inspiring design work presented in an upfront manner. Instead of wrapping all the work up in a complex and overbearing design that reduces the impact of the work, they let the work speak for itself.

By using their work as the focus of their sites, artists reinforce the idea that they are awesome at what they do. Surely, the people interested in hiring these artists appreciate when their work

is presented in a simple and elegant way. There is no fluff; they get straight to the point. They seem to say, "Here is what I have done. Love it or hate it." In the end, your work speaks volumes about your abilities, and if you have huge talent like the people featured in this section, why not cut to the chase?

These sites remind us that the work itself makes a portfolio site shine, so it may not be necessary to spend all that time on a crazy concept. If you have the work, keep it simple and just lay it on the line. Your portfolio will be easier to maintain, and your clients will thank you.

A prime example of this style is the Van Honing portfolio site. The vast major-

ity of the design space is devoted to the portfolio. There is no unnecessary text, no filler and no frivolous design. Viewers who open this page are overwhelmed by the artist's work and instantly get an impression of the type of work he does. In this case, thumbnails draw the viewer into larger images. In contrast, sites like Designgraphy use huge images of the artwork to show it off. This can be a great way to facilitate simpler consumption of the portfolio. By having larger images already on display, a visitor need not click through the site searching for them. This streamlines the viewing process and literally overpowers the visitor with one great image after another.

http://www.vanhoning.nl

http://designgraphy.com

http://www.danielsantiago.com

http://www.mattmo.com

http://www.jp33.com

http://www.wrecked.nu

http://adellecharles.com

http://www.sergiojuncos.com

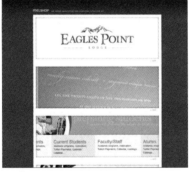

http://www.pixelshop.org

http://chromogenic.net

http://www.collision-theory.com

http://www.dnna.net

03

Nature Food Old Paper Grass Wood Clouds Splatters Workplace Print Imitation Location-Based Extreme Theme

SITES BY THEME

Creating a theme for a site can be one of the most exciting paths to take a design down. Unlike styles, themes are almost always connected to specific imagery. Some themes are subtle, others are over the top, but they all provide a path of inspiration that allows us to focus our ideas. Interestingly, by reducing our options, we find an infinite amount of them. Take, for example, a workplace theme. Until such a theme was decided upon, paper clips likely had no place in design. But now, paper clips and other workplace items are potential assets to be put to use. This sort of inspiration tends to be contagious and downright fun. Just remember to select your theme carefully, as it shapes the message you are communicating.

NATURE

The web is a technical, hard-edged place, if only because it is a programmer's paradise. One great way to escape this digital trap is to incorporate elements from the real world that cannot exist online. By working elements from nature into a design, the user is encouraged to associate it with the comfort of nature.

As with many design elements, nature-based themes can set the entire mood of a site. The trick is to use this atmosphere to communicate an important message about the site's content. Why does the design need to feel natural? Is it simply to make the user more comfortable? Or better yet, is it to communicate something about a product? After all, if the site is natural and comfortable, perhaps the product is as well.

There seem to be three main styles of implementing nature in design. First, there is the silhouette. This creates a

beautiful effect that can be contrasted by a colorful background. Second, there is straight photography, which is often used as a background, creating a beautiful platform to build on. Third, there are illustrated elements from nature. This is probably the most difficult style to implement but, as usual, the hardest path often leads to the most distinct results.

The 3000k site is a fun example of the use of nature in design. Here the metaphor for growth hits the viewer over the head. This firm is intent on helping its clients develop and grow, and the visual representation of growth communicates this. It is remarkable how this one image can support the firm's mission so well.

A great demonstration of the illustration approach is on the 9 Grados blog. The mushroom-themed header of this site is a unique and powerful image that is not easily forgotten. Every time

I see this image among a group of others it stands out. Wouldn't we all love for every design we create to make this kind of impression? Ultimately the idea is rather simple, but is it ever effective.

And we cannot forget the silhouette, which is a very popular approach. Perhaps the biggest appeal of the silhouette is that it enables the designer to include elements of nature and to draw on those connotations without having such visually complex elements. Elements from nature tend to be visually complex and can overpower the content of a site. Take a look at Grow Interactive to get an idea. Sure, the nature elements aren't pure silhouettes, but they are minimized and nearly solid in color. They frame the site and its content and provide atmosphere without distracting the viewer from the site content. A wonderful balance has been achieved.

http://www.3000k.com

http://www.thisisgrow.com

http://www.9grados.com/blog

http://mezzanineapp.com/blog

http://www.zachklein.com

http://www.bensky.co.uk

http://www.hrasti.com

http://www.holdsworthdesign.com

http://www.jochemvanwetten.nl

http://www.ysprod.com

http://www.godfarm.org

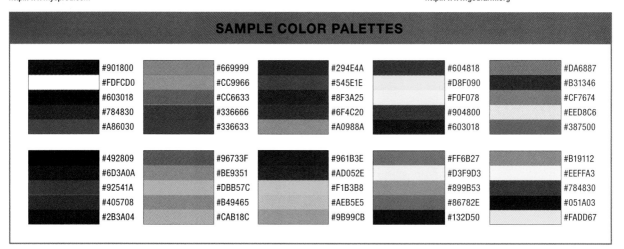

SAMPLE COLOR PALETTES

#901800	#669999	#294E4A	#604818	#DA6887
#FDFCD0	#CC9966	#545E1E	#D8F090	#B31346
#603018	#CC6633	#8F3A25	#F0F078	#CF7674
#784830	#336666	#6F4C20	#904800	#EED8C6
#A86030	#336633	#A0988A	#603018	#387500
#492809	#96733F	#961B3E	#FF6B27	#B19112
#6D3A0A	#BE9351	#AD052E	#D3F9D3	#EEFFA3
#92541A	#DBB57C	#F1B3B8	#899B53	#784830
#405708	#B49465	#AEB5E5	#86782E	#051A03
#2B3A04	#CAB18C	#9B99CB	#132D50	#FADD67

084

FOOD

Typically, food is used as a design element for either its literal or metaphoric connection to the site topic. But what is the purpose of this element, and how can it be put to good use?

My first suggestion is to forget stock photography—at least in its default form. As usual, let's look at an example to get the gist of this. The Pear Hosting sites uses various pears to communicate its packages in a playful way. Most importantly, they use illustrated pears. Why does this matter so much? Well, a photo probably would have felt pretty lame. Instead, these simple illustrations communicate the idea that the hosting company is not your typical shop. This playful presentation sets them apart as a distinct company. It shows that they

have a good attitude and like to have fun, and this really makes them appealing—kind of like a juicy pear.

Another site that uses food metaphorically and avoids lame stock photography is Tasty Apps. Though the cookie at the top of this site is clearly a photograph, it is clipped out and meshed into the site in a way that escapes the typical stock photo feel. This simple design element connects with the name of the site, but more importantly it reflects the appeal of the applications available on the site. Connecting applications with tasty chocolate cookies cannot be a bad thing. And again, the theme of the site is fun and playful, making people feel happy enough to spend a few bucks!

http://www.pearhosting.com

http://www.tastyapps.com

http://www.emanuelblagonic.com

http://www.kristinejanssen.com

http://www.jasonlimon.com

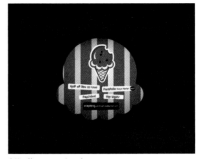

http://www.postmodernsong.org

SAMPLE COLOR PALETTES

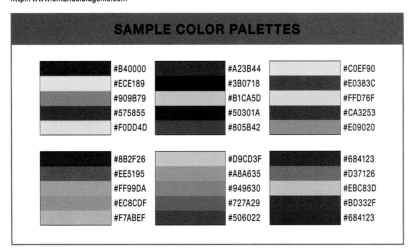

#B40000	#A23B44	#C0EF90
#ECE189	#3B0718	#E0383C
#909B79	#B1CA5D	#FFD76F
#575855	#50301A	#CA3253
#F0DD4D	#805B42	#E09020

#8B2F26	#D9CD3F	#684123
#EE5195	#A8A635	#D37126
#FF99DA	#949630	#EBC83D
#EC8CDF	#727A29	#BD332F
#F7ABEF	#506022	#684123

OLD PAPER

Using old paper products in your design is a great way to generate atmosphere and to cut through the technical muck. We all have a connection with paper. We use it all the time, and we don't associate it with the computer as much as with a tangible object, so paper can be used to create a comfortable, organic feel.

My first suggestion is to step away from the computer and see what you find. Root through an attic, a basement or the old books at a library. You are bound to uncover some incredible pieces of paper you could scan for your design. In other words, there is no need to fake it. Don't be tempted to create a hokey paper texture in Adobe Photoshop just because it seems easy. Your design will be much more powerful if you just take the steps to give it life.

For a more subtle usage let's turn to the Shut Theory site, where we find a blog with a large paper background. The page is loaded with content which, when combined with the paper background, lends itself to a newspaper feel. This is not a bad connotation for a blog, if you think about it. The writing on the site appears to be formal and in-depth, so connecting itself with a real newspaper only serves to enhance its authority. And at the same time, the little splatter in the top left helps it avoid an overly corporate feel. So the design gains authority from the newspaper, yet it avoids negative connotations by making the site clearly a grassroots operation.

Paperworks has used this element in the most literal way possible. They sell paper, and the paper used in the design connects with that. Sometimes being literal is good, especially on the web where users have such short attention spans.

http://shut.elmota.com

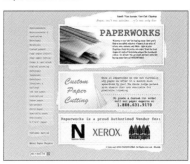

http://paperworks.com

http://www.switchinteractive.com

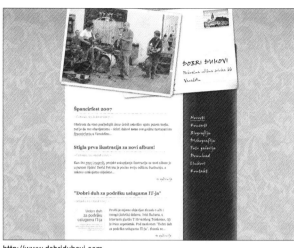

http://www.dobriduhovi.com

http://www.alterform.com

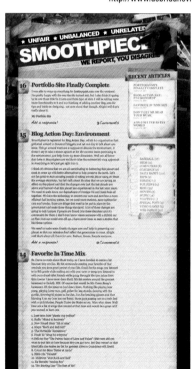

http://www.smoothpiece.net

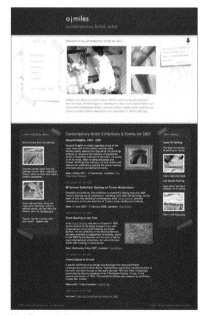

http://www.ajmiles.net

http://www.pilarpunzano.com

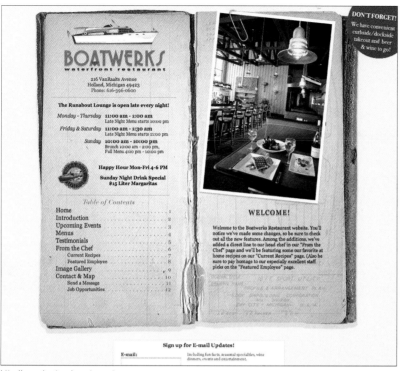

http://www.boatwerksrestaurant.com

http://www.johnphillipslive.com

http://www.plankdesign.com/en

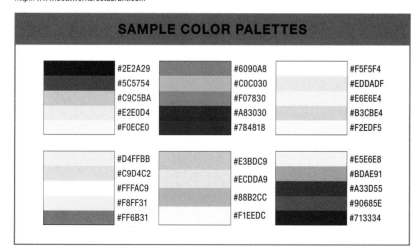

SAMPLE COLOR PALETTES

#2E2A29	
#5C5754	
#C9C5BA	
#E2E0D4	
#F0ECE0	

#6090A8	
#C0C030	
#F07830	
#A83030	
#784818	

#F5F5F4	
#EDDADF	
#E6E6E4	
#B3CBE4	
#F2EDF5	

#D4FFBB	
#C9D4C2	
#FFFAC9	
#F8FF31	
#FF6B31	

#E3BDC9	
#ECDDA9	
#88B2CC	
#F1EEDC	

#E5E6E8	
#BDAE91	
#A33D55	
#90685E	
#713334	

GRASS

The use of grass in design is relatively common—not so common as to be trendy, but it is definitely a pattern that exists. It is rather obvious when to use this design element and when not to.

There are two clear reasons to use this design element. First is the literal use. Many sites have incorporated grass into their design because it simply fits the topic of the site. Sometimes being overly literal can get annoying, but in this case it just takes a beautiful design element that happens to help communicate the purpose of the site. There is nothing wrong with rapidly communicating the

purpose of a site to visitors, and this is just the case with sites such as Pup-Style. This site is all about dogs and their accessories. The grass background calls to mind the place dogs love best—the outdoors. This is pretty literal, yet it isn't an obvious cliché. This site could have turned out cheesy. Instead, the grass background adds a beautiful style to the site and really defines the overall feel.

The second reason to use grass as a design element is to draw on its connotations to create an atmosphere that says something about a site. Grass is closely tied to the design elements of nature and

green, both of which have very pleasant connotations. By pulling in the grassy elements, these sites have warm and welcoming environments. Take a look at the Unstructure site. The first thing you notice is that it strongly resembles the PupStyle site. Although these two sites have a similar look and feel, their purpose and resulting message are very different. While PupStyle uses grass to give the viewer thoughts of puppies, Unstructure does so to generate a sense of freshness. In this case, even the scent of grass comes into play as it ties into the designer aesthetic on the Unstructure site.

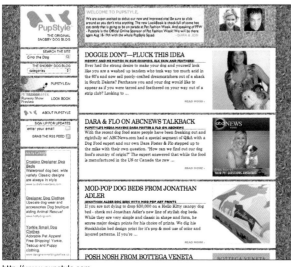

http://www.pupstyle.com

http://www.unstructure.com

http://www.freshbrew.com

http://www.designtrance.com

http://www.craig-russell.co.uk

http://www.backfrog.com

http://www.ustvarjalko.si

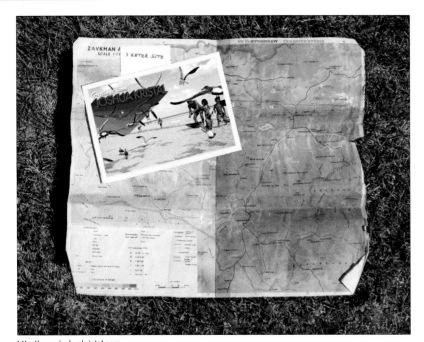

http://www.joshuakristal.com

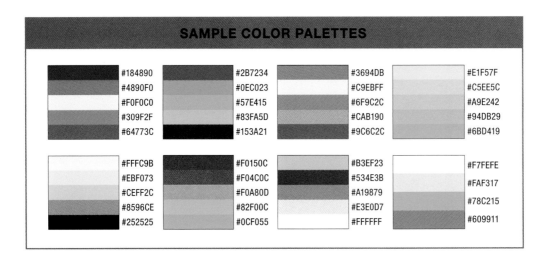

http://www.logicalbinary.com

SAMPLE COLOR PALETTES

#184890	#2B7234	#3694DB	#E1F57F
#4890F0	#0EC023	#C9EBFF	#C5EE5C
#F0F0C0	#57E415	#6F9C2C	#A9E242
#309F2F	#83FA5D	#CAB190	#94DB29
#64773C	#153A21	#9C6C2C	#6BD419

#FFFC9B	#F0150C	#B3EF23	#F7FEFE
#EBF073	#F04C0C	#534E3B	#FAF317
#CEFF2C	#F0A80D	#A19879	#78C215
#8596CE	#82F00C	#E3E0D7	#609911
#252525	#0CF055	#FFFFFF	

WOOD

Generally, wood is used on the web for aesthetic purposes more than anything else ... or is there more to it than that? It could be used to disconnect from the technical nature of the web and instead associate with more earthly, comfortable things. Whatever the reason, one thing is for sure: You will want to work on that fine photo of wood with a bit of Adobe Photoshop magic to transform the image into something that fits a site beautifully. The wood in the following sample sites appears to have been adjusted to ensure a perfect fit with the site design. As with any element, take great care with your wood photo to achieve a unified design.

Perhaps the most important things to consider when using wood in your layout are the connotations and atmosphere created by various types of wood. For example, the ISO50 site feels warm and comfortable like an old basement with wood paneling. This is appropriate considering some of the work the artist produces, with its vintage flowing stripes.

The use of wood on the Electric Pulp site certainly contributes to the site's designer feel. It has a rustic aesthetic, yet it remains clear that this is a top-rate firm that knows how to create beautiful work, and they are probably great fun to work with. This balance between hip, trendy, reliable and fun is crucial to attract large clients who want fresh ideas but who also want to work with a shop that isn't going to make more work for them.

Draft.Media and Kanaly Design, on the other hand, use wood in a wonderfully modern way, as though the site were a highly polished piece of furniture. This high-class atmosphere contrasts with the down-to-earth feel of the Grant Helton site.

http://iso50.com

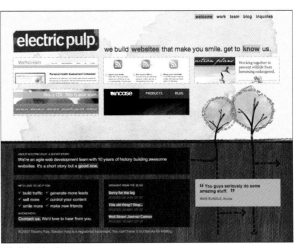

http://electricpulp.com

http://www.draftmedia.de

http://kanalydesign.com

http://skullsandcandy.com

http://granthelton.com

http://www.mondayrunner.com

http://www.capitolmedia.com

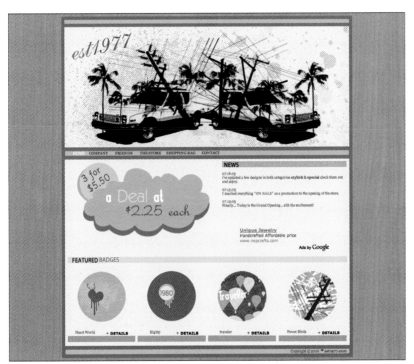

http://www.est1977.com

http://www.delicious-monster.com

SAMPLE COLOR PALETTES

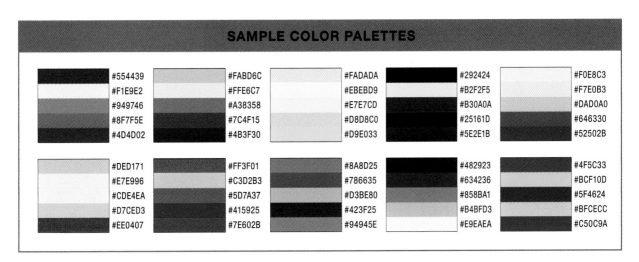

#554439	#FABD6C	#FADADA	#292424	#F0E8C3
#F1E9E2	#FFE6C7	#EBEBD9	#B2F2F5	#F7E0B3
#949746	#A38358	#E7E7CD	#B30A0A	#DAD0A0
#8F7F5E	#7C4F15	#D8D8C0	#25161D	#646330
#4D4D02	#4B3F30	#D9E033	#5E2E1B	#52502B
#DED171	#FF3F01	#8A8D25	#482923	#4F5C33
#E7E996	#C3D2B3	#786635	#634236	#BCF10D
#CDE4EA	#5D7A37	#D3BE80	#858BA1	#5F4624
#D7CED3	#415925	#423F25	#B4BFD3	#BFCECC
#EE0407	#7E602B	#94945E	#E9EAEA	#C50C9A

CLOUDS

Imagery is a potent tool that always comes loaded with connotations and subtle meanings. It may not seem like there is much to imagery as simple as clouds, yet this is entirely untrue. Clouds can be found on many sites on the web, and this small grouping of them uses clouds in a significant way. All of these sites rely on this element in clear and intentional ways.

Amazingly, the majority of the samples use cloud photographs as background images. White and blue skies aren't too high of a contrast and work remarkably well in this backstage role. In fact, they look rather gorgeous. Even the weakest of the samples has a simple, appealing beauty. Perhaps this is where the conno-

tations come in. Who doesn't love a sunny day with a few white clouds floating in the air? The imagery creates an atmosphere of happiness, which is a very good thing. You will notice that none of these sites has gray storm clouds because that would create a much different feel and serve a totally different purpose.

So what is the point? White clouds set a happy, safe mood. They are relaxing and communicate an eco-friendly feel. They aren't implicitly eco-oriented, but they certainly have a natural, healthy feel. In this way, all these sites have employed clouds to set the mood and establish expectations within the viewer.

The warm and welcoming mood on sites such as WP-design is partially

due to the cloud imagery being used. Applying a design to WordPress can be a daunting task. In this case, setting a safe and friendly atmosphere is a fantastic idea. Helping a client make tough things simple is always a good thing. In this way the use of cloud imagery has been effectively used to reinforce a key message.

Another fine example of a site that creates a safe mood for the sake of overcoming a complex topic is Mac 3D Software. Any software related to 3D functionality is expected to be complicated. So the real key to this site and its design is to assure the potential user that it isn't as daunting as expected.

http://wp-design.org

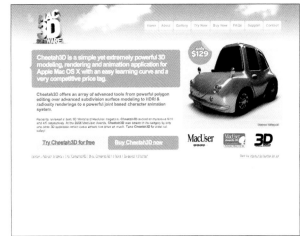

http://www.mac3dsoftware.com

http://www.nuage-et-nougatine.com

http://www.bayoukidsdirectory.com

http://www.friendsofheathergrossman.com

http://meehantherapy.com

http://www.redchess.com

SAMPLE COLOR PALETTES

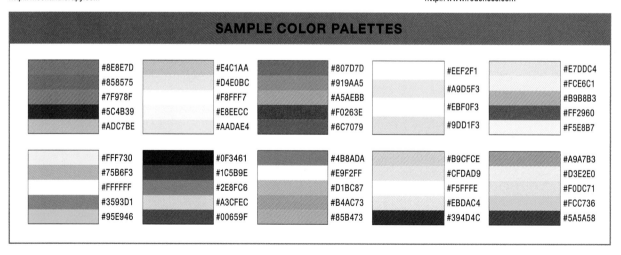

#8E8E7D	#E4C1AA	#807D7D	#EEF2F1	#E7DDC4
#858575	#D4E0BC	#919AA5	#A9D5F3	#FCE6C1
#7F978F	#F8FFF7	#A5AEBB	#EBF0F3	#B9B8B3
#5C4B39	#E8EECC	#F0263E	#9DD1F3	#FF2960
#ADC7BE	#AADAE4	#6C7079		#F5E8B7

#FFF730	#0F3461	#4B8ADA	#B9CFCE	#A9A7B3
#75B6F3	#1C5B9E	#E9F2FF	#CFDAD9	#D3E2E0
#FFFFFF	#2E8FC6	#D1BC87	#F5FFFE	#F0DC71
#3593D1	#A3CFEC	#B4AC73	#EBDAC4	#FCC736
#95E946	#00659F	#85B473	#394D4C	#5A5A58

SPLATTERS

Drips, sprays and splatters are fun design elements found on sites covering a diverse range of topics. It is easy to confuse this with the distressed style. The two are somewhat related and can even be combined in a design, but they easily stand as two distinct styles.

Sure, sites like Fendyzaidan could easily fit into the distressed category; but take a look at Producemedia, which has managed to work this bit of chaos into its ultra-clean designs. Most of the sites, though, seem to strike a balance between the clean designer feel and the ultra-distressed feel. Sites such as Organic Level show this combo in action.

So what is the message behind the drips? Mostly they seem to convey a raw, urban style. Consider the site Pit Stop

Radio: Without the pink splatter, the site would be clean and minimal. Instead, the pink splatter brings a rough edge to the site, which creates a stronger connection with its intended audience.

An example of using splatters to communicate a profession is the Drew Warkentin site. Here the colorful splatter is associated with paint and all things creative, which is most likely what the design intended.

This style can also be used in extremely subtle ways. In the case of MyOnlyWorkingEye, a slight drip has been added to the top left of the page to highlight the fact that they are accepting new clients. For obvious reasons, this is important information.

http://fendyzaidan.blogspot.com

http://www.producemedia.com

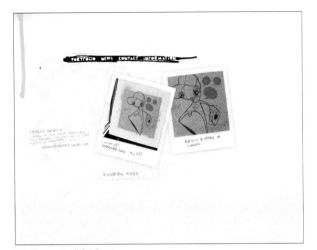

http://www.organiclevel.com

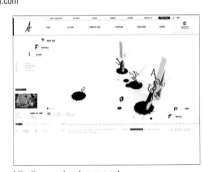

http://www.drewwarkentin.com

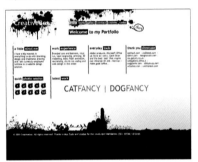

http://www.creativebox.ro

http://www.pitstopradio.be

http://www.artworksgroup.net

http://www.myonlyworkingeye.co.uk

http://www.janbrasna.com

http://www.latelier-web.fr

http://www.peminoz.com

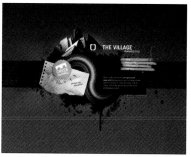

http://www.thevillage.nl

http://www.km4042.de

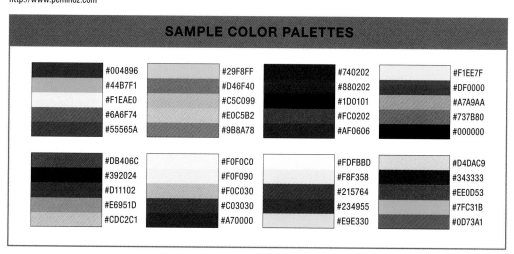

SAMPLE COLOR PALETTES

#004896
#44B7F1
#F1EAE0
#6A6F74
#55565A

#29F8FF
#D46F40
#C5C099
#E0C5B2
#9B8A78

#740202
#880202
#1D0101
#FC0202
#AF0606

#F1EE7F
#DF0000
#A7A9AA
#737B80
#000000

#DB406C
#392024
#D11102
#E6951D
#CDC2C1

#F0F0C0
#F0F090
#F0C030
#C03030
#A70000

#FDFBBD
#F8F358
#215764
#234955
#E9E330

#D4DAC9
#343333
#EE0D53
#7FC31B
#0D73A1

WORKPLACE

The idea of using workplace items in a web design probably stems from the fact that most people sit around all day surrounded by this junk! Paper clips, Post-its and pushpins seem to be the most popular items. At first glance incorporating workplace items on a site may seem like a pointless thing to do, purely for aesthetics. However, as with many elements, it is easy to find useful applications for these design flourishes.

Paper clips are similar to badges, except that paper clips accomplish their task in a subtle way. Designers can use paper clips in such a way that they appear to be holding some other element on top of the page. This creates the illusion of depth and pushes the element it is holding forward, emphasizing it. This is not nearly as bold as a badge, but it works just the same. It draws attention to some element of the page. Directing attention around a page is an important consideration and can certainly be used to the designer's advantage.

A perfect example of using office supplies to create hierarchy is on the Erik Mazzone site. Its large, bold purpose statement quickly tells users what the site represents, and the paper clip helps to highlight this statement. The angular positioning of the statement helps to make it look paper-clipped and attracts even more attention, pushing it higher in the hierarchy.

As with pretty much any other design element, the overall unification of the design is of critical importance. Designs that lack unification tend to feel unpolished and ineffective. A great example of a unified design is the seyDesign site. It has an office theme, and everything flows together perfectly. The corkboard background creates a terrific foundation to tie the site together. It essentially gives the office supplies a place to exist.

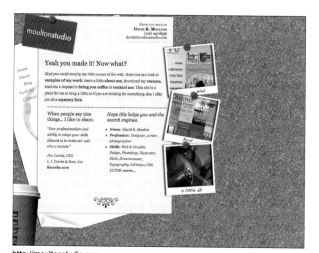

http://moultonstudio.com

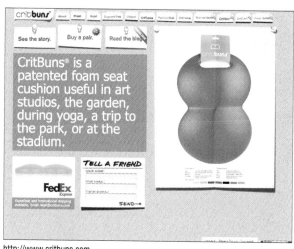

http://www.critbuns.com

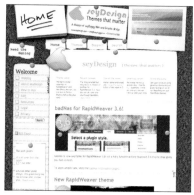

http://www.seydesign.com

http://sunsad.de

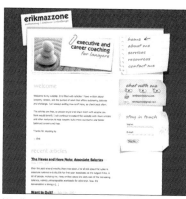

http://www.erikmazzone.com

http://www.dpivision.com

http://www.teamviget.com

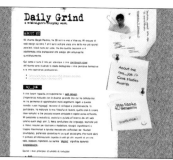

http://www.dailygrind.it

http://www.itisblank.com

http://www.tipoos.com

http://www.untiedshoes.com

SAMPLE COLOR PALETTES

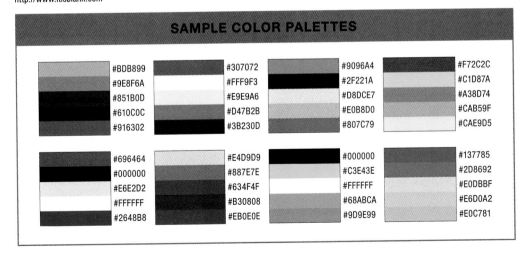

#BDB899	#307072
#9E8F6A	#FFF9F3
#851B0D	#E9E9A6
#610C0C	#D47B2B
#916302	#3B230D

#9096A4	#F72C2C
#2F221A	#C1D87A
#D8DCE7	#A38D74
#E0B8D0	#CAB59F
#807C79	#CAE9D5

#696464	#E4D9D9
#000000	#887E7E
#E6E2D2	#634F4F
#FFFFFF	#B30808
#2648B8	#EB0E0E

#000000	#137785
#C3E43E	#2D8692
#FFFFFF	#E0DBBF
#68ABCA	#E6D0A2
#9D9E99	#E0C781

PRINT IMITATION

The idea of imitating the print format on the web presumably stems from designers who are used to and comfortable with print design. Items such as portfolio pieces, writing samples and photographs that work well in print may also have contributed to this idea. The printed form has many beautiful aspects that are tempting to duplicate in a digital medium. As such, print imitation often pops up in web design.

The imitation of print can serve a purpose beyond the aesthetic. Namely, it can clue the viewer in on the purpose of a site. Print imitation would work well for a restaurant's menu site, a newspaper theme for a news site, and a sketchbook site for an illustrator. What results from its use is a set of literal connotations.

This style is most commonly used to create the look and feel of an online book. This can take on countless forms, one of which can be found on the Lime site. There is a great deal of beauty added to the presentation of the portfolio by placing it in a book. Another similar example can be found on Graynode, where again we find a book-styled portfolio. This style of layout requires a bit more effort to navigate, but the end result is a site that is as much an experience as it is informational. The owners are proving they can create an experience for the user that is distinct and memorable.

Certainly this is part of the portfolio's purpose in the first place. Consequently, the presentation becomes as much a part of the message as the content.

A very different rendition of this style comes in the form of a newspaper. One such site can be found at Gapers Block. On this site, the connotations of a newspaper are drawn upon to elevate the perceived quality and authority of the site's content. Newspapers traditionally have a more legitimate level of writing than the wild west of the Internet. This site has changed the perception of its content simply through its style of presentation. This is a powerful technique used rather nicely.

http://www.lime.ee

http://www.graynode.com

http://www.gapersblock.com

http://nationalgazette.org

http://www.feaverish.com

http://www.cirut.pl

http://www.rosefu.net

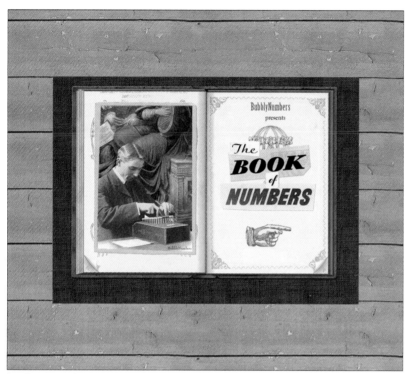

http://www.book-of-numbers.com

http://www.e-knjige.net

http://savremenaginekologija.com

SAMPLE COLOR PALETTES

	#E6A93F		#BB7534		#E2CBB2			
	#EBE1EC		#A82114		#F5E6CC			
	#523220		#72170E		#E2145F			
	#F1B579		#A0AD6C		#5FC9DF			
	#DD512B		#E7EECE		#EBE2C2			

#15AAF0		#181818		#111111
#18B6FF		#E0DCC0		#BDAF80
#44C4FF		#880010		#FEFFF8
#FF44AD		#686860		#98B7BA
#FFFF44		#C8BCA0		#5D3B2F

LOCATION-BASED

Communicating quickly with users on the web is a major challenge. Combine low attention spans with an endless supply of options, and the chance of connecting with visitors rapidly shrinks. One powerful way to communicate quickly with users is to establish an interesting environment for the site. Pulling users into the world of the site creates a new experience for them. The atmosphere of the location-based site can help explain the site's purpose and draw in users. Although this method runs the risk of complicating the viewing experience, it can also be a very effective hook.

One way to approach location-based style is to make a virtual world. Creating an entirely virtual version of a physical location is challenging but it can be tackled in a number of ways—some more literal than others. Smart photography use is a good way to use this

technique and avoid complex three-dimensional renderings. One such example is the Romain Gruner site. This site is obviously based on three-dimensional models and required major effort to produce. This idea of creating a virtual environment for the user to explore is not new, yet this site feels fresh and unique. Location-based style has this ability. The Romain Gruner site takes the notion of creating an experience for the user to a very literal level.

A second way to achieve location-based style is to make the site look and feel like a desktop. This method is similar to creating a virtual world in that it makes viewers feel as though they are in a location. However, the desktop theme produces a very distinct set of results. One such result is that it draws the visitor into a presumably private place. Take a look at the Idesyns site.

This small environment invites users into the creator's world. By doing so, it feels more intimate and sincere. The beauty of such an environment is that it doesn't require complex three-dimensional models. This particular site was built by piecing elements together to create the illusion of space, almost in collage style. Another interesting take on this idea can be found on Mood Builder. This amazing site uses a nonphotographic style to establish a playful mood and entice users into the space.

A third approach to location-based style is to draw the viewer into a fantasy world. Such is the case with the Lumus site, which has a science fiction feel. The site's creativity serves it well since its purpose is to sell creative services. The Lumus site instantly communicates the quality of work customers can expect from this firm.

http://idesyns.com

http://www.romaingruner.com

http://www.thelume.com

http://www.bullseyecreative.net

http://www.moodbuilder.com

http://www.netsuperstar.com

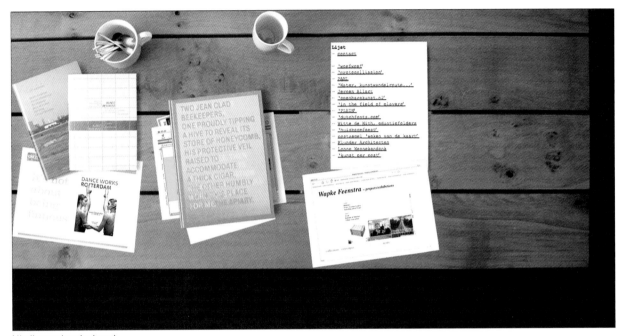

http://www.arienneboelens.nl

http://astrostudios.com

http://piotrowskimichal.com

http://onemillionpod.com

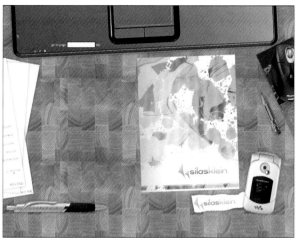

http://www.silasklein.com

http://www.foxie.ru

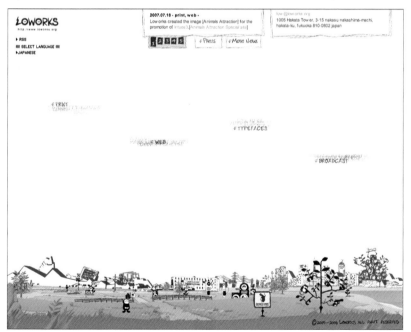

http://www.loworks.org

http://www.notsosimpleton.com/TheFragileCircus

http://www.iconinc.com.au

EXTREME THEME

At times, web design can be the most frustrating endeavor. Creating the ultimate design can be challenging and maddening. I have observed that a design theme almost always makes the process easier. Settling on a theme as opposed to a design style can really get the ideas flowing. Instead of setting out to make a shiny or distressed site, consider themes that would support the site's topic. Often, themes sound ridiculous (and they usually are), but once they are implemented, they are fun and really bring a site to life.

For example, Indigo6 turned its basic black site into a clever theme-based site. Instead of a plain content-driven design, its airline theme creates a fun atmosphere. The user can't help

but wonder what the site holds and is drawn in to explore further. As a result, the site becomes an experience. I can just imagine the design meeting for this site. Someone says, "Let's make it nice and clean." Then someone else says, "Hey, what if it was like you were on a plane and there was a flight attendant?" Surely someone scoffed at the proposal, but the most radical ideas can deliver the most terrific results. In this case, the entire airline industry becomes a source of inspiration.

If there is one industry that is highly prone to boring web design, it is the trucking industry. Yet the Visit Cascadia site has been completely transformed by the use of a theme. Sometimes, dull topics present the best opportunity for

success. A willingness to play on stereotypes and just have fun enabled the designers behind this site to explore some thematic ways of presenting some anticlimactic content. So instead of a completely boring and forgettable design, they created a unique site with an unforgettable theme.

I can imagine someone reading this and saying, "Sure, that sounds nice, but it doesn't apply to my big, stuffy, boring, corporate client." On the contrary! Any site can have a theme, but it doesn't have to be extreme. Extreme themes are good for showing the power of the tool. But even corporate customers have a story to tell and a need to communicate with and entice visitors. Themes can do all of this and more.

http://www.visitcascadia.com

http://www.indigo6.com/site2006

http://www.dizzain.com

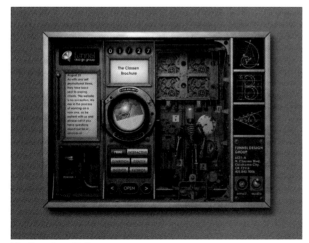

http://www.funneldesigngroup.com

http://www.inyourelement.org

http://www.webtreasure.eu

http://egypt.ebeling.ee/panoramas

http://saizenmedia.com

http://www.joblankenburg.com/english

04

SITES BY COLOR

Color selection is an important step in the design process that is often overlooked—if not altogether ignored. Selecting colors based on personal preference or just out of habit is far from the desired approach. Every color and color combination has a distinct set of meanings. These meanings can be put to use in an endless variety of ways. But ultimately, the reasoning behind color selection should be founded in the purpose of the design. Sure, at times it is heavily controlled by a client's specifications, but even within such limitations there is great power in the way the colors are used and in what colors are used alongside them. Hopefully, by seeing sites categorized by color use, you will discover each color's potential and be spurred to adopt a deeper selection process. Each color does, in fact, have powerful connotations that will become evident as we make our way through the rainbow.

PINK

The color pink typically symbolizes love, beauty and femininity. It also tends to be an exciting, energetic and stylish color. Despite the assumption that the color pink must be a feminine color, it has found its way into many unexpected sites. It is interesting to see how such a feminine color can be used in ways that easily avoid any such connotations. In fact, it seems to be a rather popular color among male designers.

A fine example of how pink can be used without being overly connected to all things feminine is the MacMinds site. It has a stylish pink and gray layout that is more fashionable than anything else. The site's design and color palette cleverly play into the hip appeal of Apple products by using a clean design com-bined with a single solid color. This is very sensible branding. Any site that wants to connect with Mac users should be on the same design level. Thus the minimal and neutral design with a single popping color is the perfect path to follow.

Another example of the stylish use of pink is the Digital Devotion site. This site has some of the same hip appeal as MacMinds but without the refined, semi-glossy feel. Here, pink has been combined with ornate floral elements. The end result is a much more urban aesthetic. The design has a vibrant life to it that contrasts with the approach used on the MacMinds site.

The Big File Box site is an example not only of how pink can avoid feminine connotations but also of how it finds its way into surprising topics. How is it that the color pink finds itself in use on a site that provides a file sharing service? It seems that in this case the color pink is an attempt to break some stereotypes surrounding such a service. Pink is not traditionally associated with technology, yet file sharing is just that. In this design the color helps distract the user from the technical hurdles of sending large files and instead makes it feel like a cool service. In this case the color pink puts a friendly face on an otherwise dull topic.

Connotations of pink: soothing, relax-ing, fresh, sensuous, restful, tranquilizing, healthy, happy, sweet, nice, playful. Also associated with passion, romance, love, innocence, marriage, health, life, sexual-ity, purity, gratitude and appreciation.

http://www.digitaldevotion.de

http://www.macminds.net

http://www.bigfilebox.com

http://blog.articlestudio.ca

http://www.foan82.com

http://www.codepink4peace.org

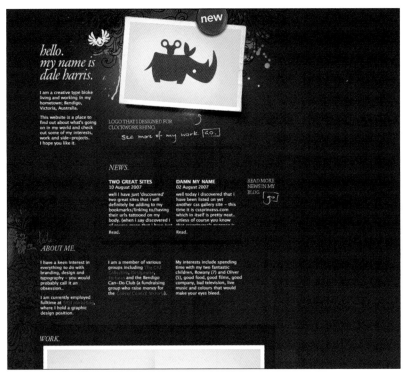

http://www.daleharris.com

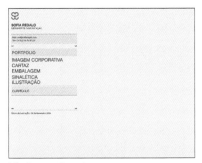

http://www.sofiaregalo.com

http://www.bowwowlondon.com

http://www.themissinglink.nl

SAMPLE COLOR PALETTES

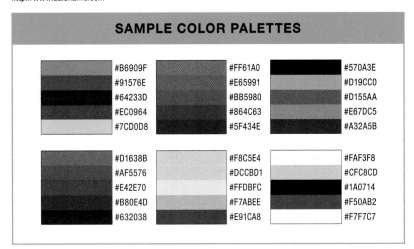

#B6909F	#FF61A0	#570A3E	
#91576E	#E65991	#D19CC0	
#64233D	#BB5980	#D155AA	
#EC0964	#864C63	#E67DC5	
#7CD0D8	#5F434E	#A32A5B	

#D1638B	#F8C5E4	#FAF3F8	
#AF5576	#DCCBD1	#CFC8CD	
#E42E70	#FFDBFC	#1A0714	
#B80E4D	#F7ABEE	#F50AB2	
#632038	#E91CA8	#F7F7C7	

118

RED

Red is an emotionally charged and remarkably powerful color. It is commonly considered the most powerful color and has extreme emotional connotations with variations from courage and love to danger and hell. Some people think that red is so tied to victory that simply wearing it can bring success. On a business website, red is bold, powerful and confident, and it strongly contrasts the neutrality of the traditional corporate blue.

Wurkit Books has made clever use of the color red. The site revolves around great quotes from books with interesting commentary on how these quotes impact real life. The intelligence of this color use is found in the fact that quotes from books are typically used for their impact and power; how appropriate is it that the color red is used to present them? The power and confidence of these quotes is enhanced by the appropriate use of red.

Standing in contrast to sites such as Wurkit Books are those like Ilas, where we find heavy use of the color. The Ilas site is exceptionally dramatic with a bold design. The power of the color red is echoed in the large and dominating headings. In this case, the confidence of red shows through as the site's confidence in its subject matter is made evident. The site has an extremely limited color palette, comprised mainly of two colors. Red is so strongly used that the addition of another color would dilute the design's effectiveness. It is interesting to see how red is used to reflect the company's confidence and authority in its field rather than to highlight a specific element of the page. By so much bold use of red, everything starts to equalize. This, of course, makes extremely bold type necessary for important site elements.

Connotations of red: trustworthy, warm, fun, sacred, hot, intense, angry, high energy, strong, aggressive, dangerous, passionate, courageous. Also associated with patriotism, conservatism, stability, success, emotion, good fortune, Valentine's Day, Christmas, power, communism, fire, blood, health, emergency, good fortune, love, heat, evil, respect and vitality.

http://www.wurkit.com

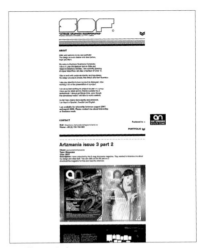

http://www.ilas.com

http://www.stephano.se

http://www.sonze.com

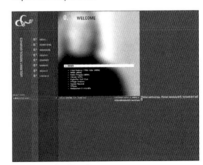

http://www.dan03.net

http://www.gearboxmedia.com

http://www.youthagainstsudoku.com

http://www.heuserkampf.com

http://hellomuller.com

SAMPLE COLOR PALETTES

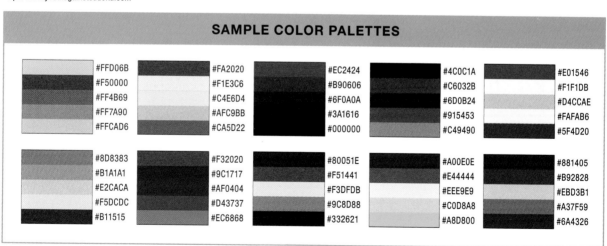

#FFD06B	#FA2020	#EC2424	#4C0C1A	#E01546
#F50000	#F1E3C6	#B90606	#C6032B	#F1F1DB
#FF4B69	#C4E6D4	#6F0A0A	#6D0B24	#D4CCAE
#FF7A90	#AFC9BB	#3A1616	#915453	#FAFAB6
#FFCAD6	#CA5D22	#000000	#C49490	#5F4D20

#8D8383	#F32020	#80051E	#A00E0E	#881405
#B1A1A1	#9C1717	#F51441	#E44444	#B92828
#E2CACA	#AF0404	#F3DFDB	#EEE9E9	#EBD3B1
#F5DCDC	#D43737	#9C8D88	#C0D8A8	#A37F59
#B11515	#EC6868	#332621	#A8D800	#6A4326

ORANGE

Orange is a fun color with distinct connotations. Luckily some of the obvious ones are easy to avoid because the color is rather flexible. For example, orange is often associated with Halloween, but as the sample sites demonstrate, this association does not pose an insurmountable obstacle. Based on my search for sites in this category, orange seems to be a less popular choice for designers. Many of the sites I browsed that made heavy use of the color struck me as sloppy and immature. This could mean that the color is more challenging to use effectively than other choices. The difficulty associated with this color choice makes the beautiful samples assembled here even more impressive.

In terms of weight, orange carries a fair amount of power. It is not quite as bold or harsh as red, yet it is not as light or soft as yellow. It conveys a friendly and inviting environment while maintaining a level of professionalism, seriousness and, quite often, youthful fun. Orange can be a very hip color.

The Designer in Action site is a great example of how orange can be extremely stylish if used well. This site uses the color in a supportive role instead of a primary one, and it demonstrates the professionalism the color can carry. By using orange in a less dominant way—less pixel space—the site avoids being too overpowering. This plays into the site's refined design and makes it fun and dynamic to look at, even if you don't speak German. You know a site is well designed when it leaves you wishing you knew a different language.

Considering the conservative stereotypes surrounding most churches, it is fun to find a beautifully designed church site using an edgy color such as orange.

The Generation Church site has made powerful use of this very nonconservative color. This is clearly a church that is focused on attracting a younger generation. The use of orange on this site presents the church in an enthusiastic and vibrant way. The fun connotations of orange shine through and create an atmosphere that appeals to a younger generation—the kind of people who surf the web to find a church home. The selection of orange in this case was a brilliant choice.

Connotations of orange: flamboyant, energetic, stimulating, sociable, friendly, balanced, enthusiastic, vibrant, active. Also associated with Thanksgiving, Halloween, autumn, nature, earth, warmth, energy, sun, health, citrus, fertility, fire, luxury and heat.

http://www.designerinaction.de

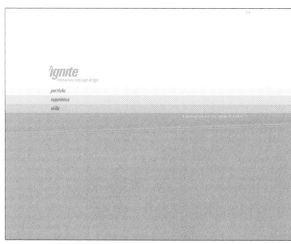

http://www.ignite-imd.com

http://www.beansbox.com

http://generationchurch.org

http://www.enhancedlabs.com

http://spousenotes.com

http://www.inmo-site.net

http://www.denyingphoenix.com

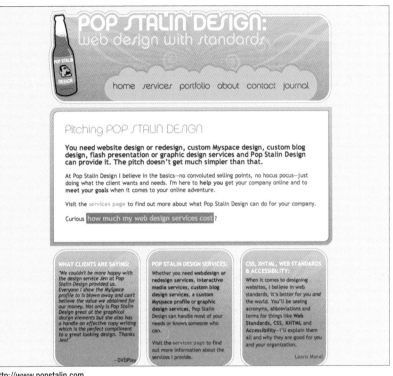

http://www.popstalin.com

SAMPLE COLOR PALETTES

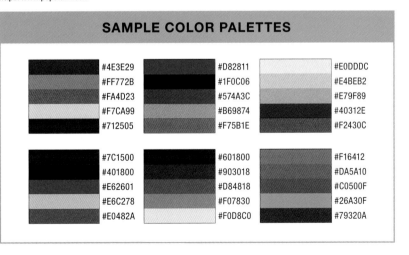

#4E3E29	#D82811
#FF772B	#1F0C06
#FA4D23	#574A3C
#F7CA99	#B69874
#712505	#F75B1E

#E0DDDC		
#E4BEB2		
#E79F89		
#40312E		
#F2430C		

#7C1500	#601800
#401800	#903018
#E62601	#D84818
#E6C278	#F07830
#E0482A	#F0D8C0

#F16412
#DA5A10
#C0500F
#26A30F
#79320A

YELLOW

Yellow is another unpopular color that finds infrequent use on the web. It is seldom used prominently in a design. All the same, yellow has some useful connotations, and it can be very effectively used. Let's look at a few samples to see what kind of meaning can be drawn from the color.

The NO!SPEC site is the first to stand out. It clearly uses yellow to reinforce its purpose, which is to warn people about the downside of accepting spec work (work you speculate will make you money, not fee-based work). The entire site is like a great big caution sign, so yellow is an appropriate color choice. Caution is one of the most common connotations of yellow, and I can't imagine another color palette being as effective on the NO!SPEC site.

Other sites like HelloBard use the color in less dramatic ways. The site seems to draw on the color yellow for abstract purposes. It is the connotations of the color that make this use appropriate. Here, yellow generates a fun, energetic, happy atmosphere, which effectively affirms the playful imagery used in the design. The color works with the illustrations to reinforce a mood and helps communicate an overall message. This is the way things are supposed to work, and the unified aesthetic results in a fantastically effective design.

Connotations of yellow: earthy, warm, fun, energizing, cheerful, healthy, hopeful, supportive, relaxed. Also associated with cowardice, nature, summer, inspiration, hazard, warning, emergency, sunshine, happiness, joy, deceit and excitement.

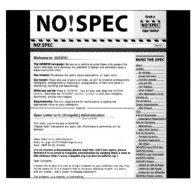

http://www.no-spec.com

http://www.hellobard.com

http://www.hive.com.au

http://www.twistsystems.co.uk

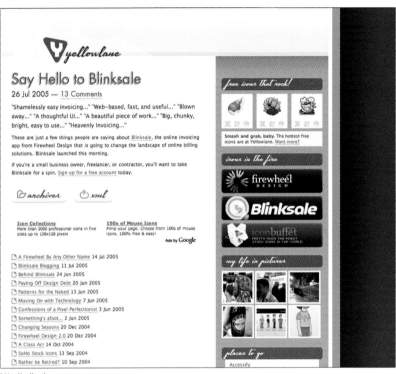

http://yellowlane.com

http://ttcrew.free.fr

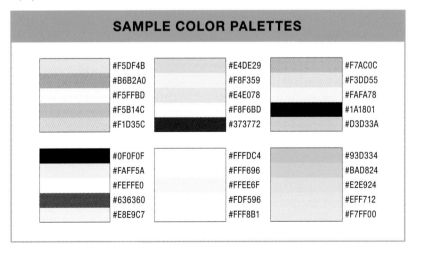

SAMPLE COLOR PALETTES

#F5DF4B	#E4DE29	#F7AC0C
#B6B2A0	#F8F359	#F3DD55
#F5FFBD	#E4E078	#FAFA78
#F5B14C	#F8F6BD	#1A1801
#F1D35C	#373772	#D3D33A
#0F0F0F	#FFFDC4	#93D334
#FAFF5A	#FFF696	#BAD824
#FEFFE0	#FFEE6F	#E2E924
#636360	#FDF596	#EFF712
#E8E9C7	#FFF8B1	#F7FF00

GREEN

The color green is another color that designers frequently rely on for its flexibility. Its primary association is with nature and the environment. Green is also closely associated with money and the idea of "proceeding," as suggested by traffic signals. The color's message can range from Irish, to financial, or even to punk. In most of the samples the use of green creates a soothing and safe feel, and many of the sites are very refreshing. This is a versatile color to be sure.

Green is very similar to brown in that it has many ways to be connected to nature, and at times it can be difficult to disconnect it from this meaning. Despite the obvious nature connotations, green is used far more often for its ability to present a topic in a fresh and light way. A perfect example of this is the website for the stats application Mint. Website

stat applications have a tradition of being technically oriented, making them complicated and hard to understand. By using the color green, the designer has suggested something different about this solution. Green presents the product in a fresh and comfortable way, subtly hinting to the visitor that it is easy to use and more than worth the low price. It is especially helpful when such connotations are actually true, which they happen to be in this case.

For a very different aesthetic created with the color green we turn to Net Profit Services. On this site we find again that green has been used as an accent color, but this time it is combined with much darker grays, which results in a hip designer aesthetic.

Quite often green is used as the primary color in a design. Such is the

case with the JamFactory site. The site is lively and fun, and the color green completely plays into this. Some artists are dark and brooding, others are light and fluffy, but this one comes across as down-to-earth and rather sensible. It is truly amazing how much you can read into people based on the color use on their websites. It certainly speaks to the importance of careful color choice for any site.

Connotations of green: soothing, relaxing, restful, organic, calming, balanced, stable, fresh. Also associated with nature, the environment, money, wealth, luck, family, fertility, harmony, health, peace, vigor, posterity, jealousy, envy, springtime, youth, humor, fun, happiness, life, growth, recycling, plants and trees.

http://www.netprofitservices.com

http://www.haveamint.com

http://www.jam-factory.com

http://www.alexpaulo.com

128

http://www.kokodigital.co.uk

http://www.thruthewoods.com

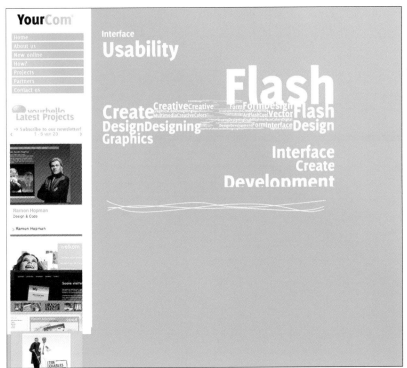

http://www.xhtmlit.com

http://www.yourcom.nl

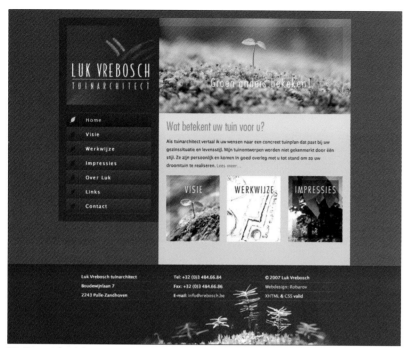

http://www.vrebosch.be

http://blogactionday.org

SAMPLE COLOR PALETTES

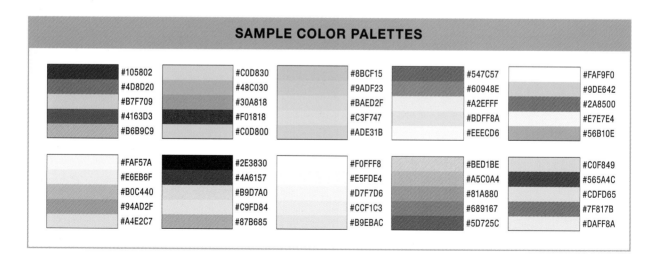

#105802	#C0D830	#8BCF15	#547C57	#FAF9F0
#4D8D20	#48C030	#9ADF23	#60948E	#9DE642
#B7F709	#30A818	#BAED2F	#A2EFFF	#2A8500
#4163D3	#F01818	#C3F747	#BDFF8A	#E7E7E4
#B6B9C9	#C0D800	#ADE31B	#EEECD6	#56B10E

#FAF57A	#2E3830	#F0FFF8	#BED1BE	#C0F849
#E6EB6F	#4A6157	#E5FDE4	#A5C0A4	#565A4C
#B0C440	#B9D7A0	#D7F7D6	#81A880	#CDFD65
#94AD2F	#C9FD84	#CCF1C3	#689167	#7F817B
#A4E2C7	#87B685	#B9EBAC	#5D725C	#DAFF8A

BLUE

The color blue is quite possibly the safest color to use for a website. It can apply to pretty much any subject matter because it is one of the most well-liked colors. Blue is calming, safe and trustworthy; it is perfect for creating a safe atmosphere on the web, where one never knows who to trust. This is especially true when the subject matter lends itself to negative or complex connotations.

Blue is passive and diplomatic. This means that although the color might support your intended message, it will not be doing so boldly. Blue can be used to create hot designs that grab the user's attention, but getting blue to pack the bold punch of red is not a likely event. The upside to this is that blue is much less abrasive. If red shouts a message, blue whispers it. This makes blue one of the safest and most conservative colors to use in web design.

Centrigy is a media company that owns several online ventures. Based on the design of their site, one would suspect that this is a sharp, high-end company. Centrigy could have designed their site using any color, but they chose blue. Their crisp, blue design supports the smart business model they espouse on their site. Centrigy is viewed as a smart, business-conscious firm, and the color blue plays into these connotations. Their modern high-end design illustrates their cutting-edge mentality, while the color blue reinforces the caution with which they approach projects. In this way, blue has been used to provide this company with a stable image in an otherwise unstable industry.

In addition to the psychological reasons for using blue, one can use it for more literal purposes. On the Maryland Media site we find a design making considerable use of the color blue. The homepage starts with a heading stating "A Clean Approach." The color blue has clean connotations that reflect this ideal, and the soothing use of subtle gradients contributes to the support of their mantra. Blue is easily connected with water, purity and an overall sense of cleanliness. Thus, the color blue plays into the studio's desire to present itself as an effective and clean design firm.

Connotations of blue: stable, trustworthy, conservative, cool, calm, strong, steadfast, friendly, confident, safe, corporate, old-fashioned, truthful, loyal, faithful, noble, scholarly, unexpected. Also associated with harmony, unity, cleanliness, power, water, trouble, intelligence, depression, defeat, cold, light, mourning, richness, superiority, technology, patriotism and sadness.

http://www.centrigy.com

http://marylandmedia.com

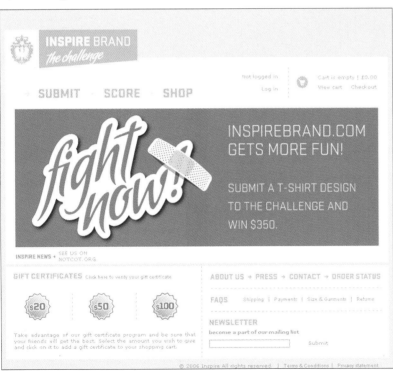

http://www.inspirebrand.com

http://www.bartelme.at

http://www.madmilk.com

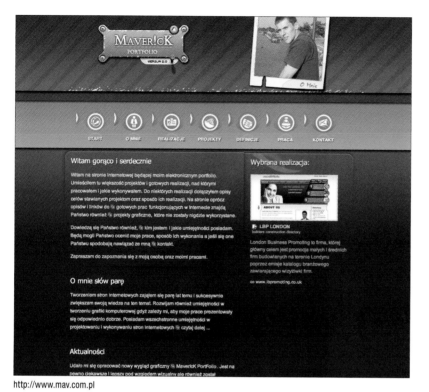

http://www.mav.com.pl

http://www.microico.com

http://michalsobel.pomeranc.cz

http://www.myquire.com

http://www.usemime.com

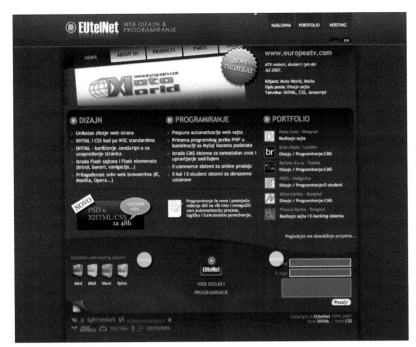

http://www.eutelnet.biz

http://emanuelfelipe.net

SAMPLE COLOR PALETTES

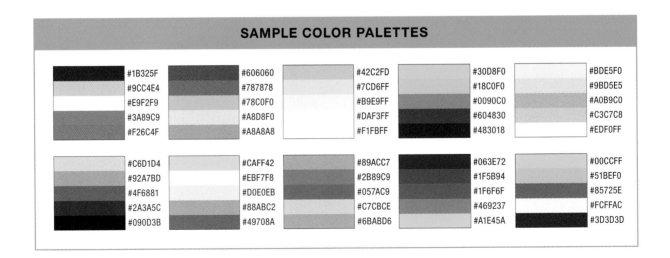

#1B325F	#606060	#42C2FD	#30D8F0	#BDE5F0	
#9CC4E4	#787878	#7CD6FF	#18C0F0	#9BD5E5	
#E9F2F9	#78C0F0	#B9E9FF	#0090C0	#A0B9C0	
#3A89C9	#A8D8F0	#DAF3FF	#604830	#C3C7C8	
#F26C4F	#A8A8A8	#F1FBFF	#483018	#EDF0FF	

#C6D1D4	#CAFF42	#89ACC7	#063E72	#00CCFF	
#92A7BD	#EBF7F8	#2B89C9	#1F5B94	#51BEF0	
#4F6881	#D0E0EB	#057AC9	#1F6F6F	#85725E	
#2A3A5C	#88ABC2	#C7CBCE	#469237	#FCFFAC	
#090D3B	#49708A	#6BABD6	#A1E45A	#3D3D3D	

134

PURPLE

Purple is one of the least used colors in web design. In fact, this section was exceedingly hard to fill and was nearly cut from the book. Perhaps this actually makes the color an interesting one to explore. Because purple is so seldom used, it represents an opportunity to tap into a less commonplace color scheme. Perhaps its infrequent use is due to some limitations or perceived problems with the color. Namely, it is often perceived as being overtly feminine. As with many stereotypes, though, this one is not true at all. Indeed, in many situations the color has very feminine overtones, but it all comes down to how you use the color and how you can leverage its effects on the viewer. And of course the samples contained here prove this point.

Pink is the close sister of purple, and it has no problem finding abundant use. This is likely because pink comes across as a more trendy color and is able to bypass its feminine connotations easily, enabling its use in a wide range of topics. Pink is the new black, while purple is, well, just purple. It seems to be a real challenge to turn purple into something less gender focused. One such example comes from a creative portfolio by Marios Tziortzis. On this site the use of purple combined with ornate gold elements creates a regal feel. This serves to elevate the perceived quality of the work contained inside the site. The purple sets off the richness of his artwork nicely.

Purple is a somewhat delicate color. Much like orange, it tends to feel sloppy and unrefined. This makes attractive sites such as Bel Koo all the more impressive. The terrific ornate background breaks up the purple tones and creates an elegant atmosphere for the site. This, combined with the smooth Bauhaus font in the logo, results in a unique and appealing design that rises above the connotations of purple and creates a pleasing visual experience.

Connotations of purple: romantic, delicate, cheerful, feminine, humble, pure. Also associated with royalty, prosperity, wealth, spirituality, Easter, wisdom, healing, nobility, justice, mystery, mourning and death.

http://marios.tziortzis.com/photoblog

http://www.tndmedia.nl

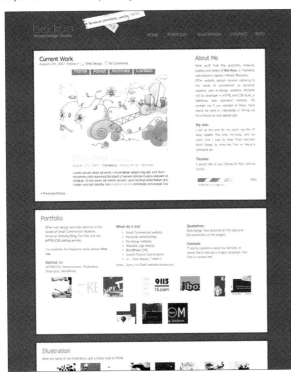

http://www.dream-design.net

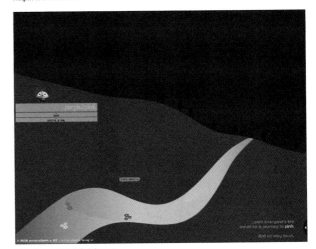

http://www.purple2pink.com

136

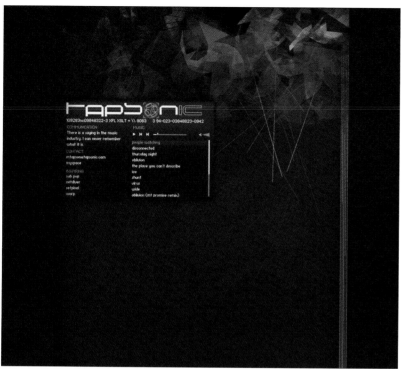

http://www.tapsonic.com

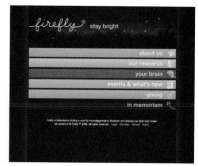

http://www.fireflyfoundation.org

http://www.espiratecnologias.com

SAMPLE COLOR PALETTES

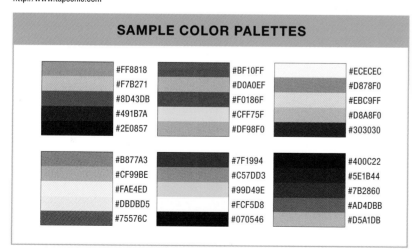

	#FF8818
	#F7B271
	#8D43DB
	#491B7A
	#2E0857

	#BF10FF
	#D0A0EF
	#F0186F
	#CFF75F
	#DF98F0

	#ECECEC
	#D878F0
	#EBC9FF
	#D8A8F0
	#303030

	#B877A3
	#CF99BE
	#FAE4ED
	#DBDBD5
	#75576C

	#7F1994
	#C57DD3
	#99D49E
	#FCF5D8
	#070546

	#400C22
	#5E1B44
	#7B2860
	#AD4DBB
	#D5A1DB

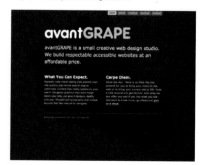

http://www.avantgrape.com

BROWN

The color brown can offer a variety of meanings to a design. One of the most obvious is its association with nature. Some sites have subject matter, such as a park or a wilderness lodge, that makes this a logical choice. In contrast, some layouts use this color to draw on its power to create a warm and friendly environment, like the Ploink!Brothers site does.

An example of good use of brown can be found on the Quo Consulting site, the online home for a creative studio. In a market saturated with options, you really have to sell yourself in the design industry, especially considering the fact that your ability to represent yourself

well reflects your ability to help clients. Quo Consulting has done just that by presenting a very conservative and safe online image. This image establishes their reliability and overall stability as an organization. It gives users the impression that working with this studio will be an easy ride, not a bumpy one led by absent-minded artists. The color brown plays into all of these ideas and serves as a key component in contributing to the marketing message of the site.

Using brown to draw on the obvious connotations of nature is the most literal use of the color. A fine example can be found on the Envirocorp Labs site. Here

we find a company that deals in water and soil testing. Brown is a logical design choice for this eco-oriented service. Upon looking at the site, it is immediately clear that it has something to do with the environment. This kind of instant recognition is exactly what designers strive for in an industry where the viewer's attention can be lost in an instant.

Connotations of brown: warm, conservative, earthy, natural, down-to-earth, wholesome, friendly. Also associated with age, nature, simplicity, dependability, health, honesty, comfort and steadiness.

http://www.quo.com.au

http://www.envirocorplabs.com

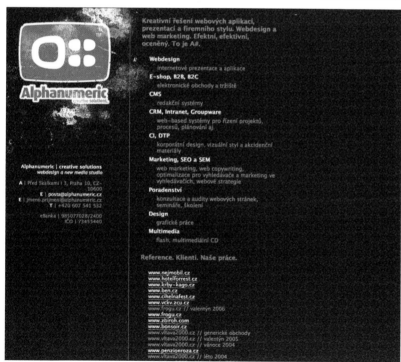

http://www.alphanumeric.cz

http://www.ploink-brothers.com

http://www.78d.se

http://www.okapistudio.com

http://www.cloigheann.com

http://www.krabi.ee

http://www.terrabaltica.lv/en

http://www.blastadvancedmedia.com

http://www.tyrcha.com

SAMPLE COLOR PALETTES

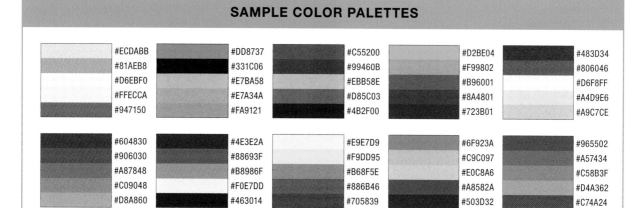

#ECDABB	#DD8737	#C55200	#D2BE04	#483D34	
#81AEB8	#331C06	#99460B	#F99802	#806046	
#D6EBF0	#E7BA58	#EBB58E	#B96001	#D6F8FF	
#FFECCA	#E7A34A	#D85C03	#8A4801	#A4D9E6	
#947150	#FA9121	#4B2F00	#723B01	#A9C7CE	

#604830	#4E3E2A	#E9E7D9	#6F923A	#965502	
#906030	#88693F	#F9DD95	#C9C097	#A57434	
#A87848	#B8986F	#B68F5E	#E0C8A6	#C58B3F	
#C09048	#F0E7DD	#886B46	#A8582A	#D4A362	
#D8A860	#463014	#705839	#503D32	#C74A24	

BLACK

Black is one of the stronger, heavier colors whose weight is nearly as powerful as that of the color red. A key difference is that black carries a weight of importance while red offers a more direct, bold punch. Both are forceful colors, but black is the more restrained of the two. Black is a strong color without the emotion and attention-grabbing quality of red.

In print it is not practical to use reversed-out text, but on the web there is a lot more flexibility. Not having to deal with how much a paper bleeds only leaves the designer to worry about more direct problems like how easy some text is to read. Legibility can be controlled through scale and font choice.

One of black's most interesting qualities is its ability to make other colors pop. Photos stand out well on black, and anything with color can really pack a punch when combined properly with black. Matt Brett's site is a fantastic example of this. The beautiful saturated colors on this site look so much richer with the black background. The color combination creates a polished, sophisticated feel.

Another site with a lot of visual impact is the Firewheel Design site. Here we find black combined with intense oranges. The Firewheel site has so much pop it appears to electrify the page. The amazing thing is that this site defies the typical connotations of black;

dark and scary images certainly don't come to mind when you browse either of these sites.

One more fantastic example of the effective use of black is the Not Only But Also site. The nice thing about this site is that it does not rely entirely on reversed-out text. It creates a wonderful balance by using black and white evenly in the design. It isn't overly dark even though it is primarily a black site.

Connotations of black: evil, powerful, mournful, strong, sophisticated, formal, conservative, serious, mysterious, sexy, rebellious, elegant, illegal, wicked, intense, mature, advanced, fashionable, stylish, chic, trendy, self-confident. Also associated with death and night.

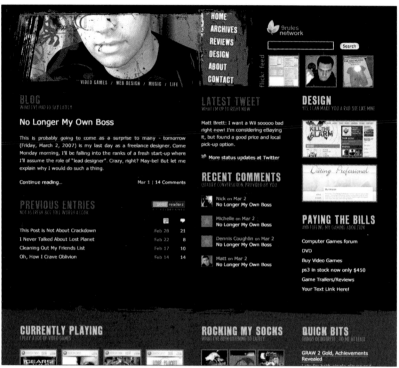

http://mattbrett.com

http://lacuria.com/movieworld

http://www.firewheeldesign.com

http://www.notonlybutalso.net

143

http://www.myvirb.net

http://ignition360.co.uk

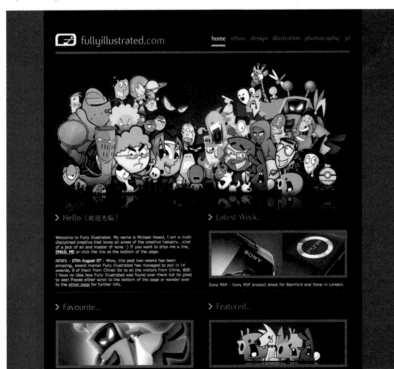

http://www.fullyillustrated.com

http://www.buzzrecruitment.co.nz

http://coda.co.za

http://www.strife.dk

http://26bits.com

SAMPLE COLOR PALETTES

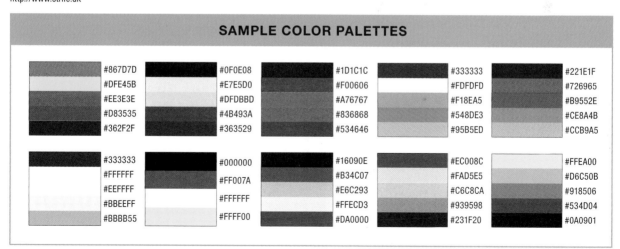

#867D7D	#0F0E08
#DFE45B	#E7E5D0
#EE3E3E	#DFDBBD
#D83535	#4B493A
#362F2F	#363529

#1D1C1C	#333333
#F00606	#FDFDFD
#A76767	#F18EA5
#836868	#548DE3
#534646	#95B5ED

#221E1F
#726965
#B9552E
#CE8A4B
#CCB9A5

#333333	#000000
#FFFFFF	#FF007A
#EEFFFF	#FFFFFF
#BBEEFF	#FFFF00
#BBBB55	

#16090E	#EC008C
#B34C07	#FAD5E5
#E6C293	#C6C8CA
#FFECD3	#939598
#DA0000	#231F20

#FFEA00
#D6C50B
#918506
#534D04
#0A0901

GRAY

Gray is a an odd color to discuss since it is defined by what it is not rather than by what it is. It is not bold, powerful or intense, and is thus neutral, disarming and often unnoticeable. Gray can be warm or cool, but it is most often completely neutral. And yet, somehow, many of the neutral variations still feel cool unless they have some solid black in them.

Gray is commonly associated with technology and can frequently be found on sites relating to such topics. There is a strong connection between stark neutral tones and modern design and technology. Perhaps this is a result of modernism's roots, which include lots of neutral colors. These stark, neutral palettes slowly became associated with technology and all things modern. (Consider the movie *2001: A Space Odyssey*, which reflects and reinforces this association.)

Portfolio and other image-heavy sites make abundant use of a neutral gray layout. Typically, the goal behind such an approach is to make the imagery stand out. One of the strengths of gray is its ability to establish hierarchy. By presenting most of a layout in gray, you can reduce the importance of certain elements in the overall design, allowing the colored elements to pop. In other words, gray can be powerful in a supporting role; it seldom takes front stage but instead gives the limelight to other, more visually dominant elements.

A fun example of a mostly gray design is that of the SnapPages site. This is a perfect demonstration of how the neutrality of gray can force other elements to pop. The intense greens look stunning on their gray backgrounds, and their priority in the hierarchy is easily established by this contrast. Also notice how stylish the gray design is and how it creates a "cool" atmosphere for the site.

Connotations of gray: stylish, chic, elegant, classy, fresh, innovative, modern, futuristic, fashionable, soft, airy, high-tech, sleek, neutral, conservative, smart, trendy, state-of-the-art, calm, comfortable. Also associated with technology, spaciousness, relaxation, peace and impartiality.

http://www.snappages.com

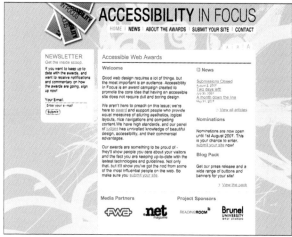

http://www.accessibilityinfocus.co.uk

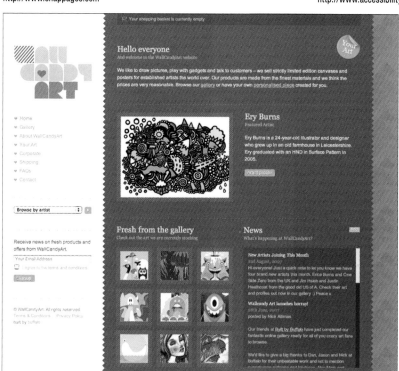

http://www.wallcandyart.co.uk

http://www.craigarmstrongonline.com

http://www.tomas-design.com

147

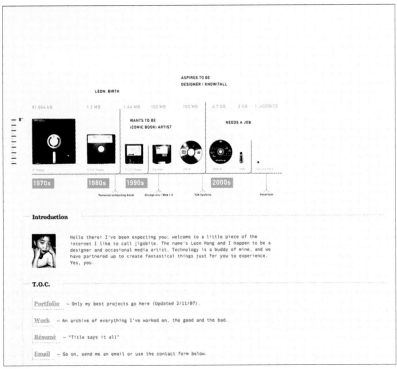

http://www.jigobite.com

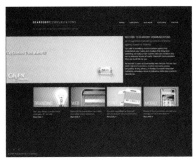

http://www.deardorffinc.com

http://www.ronniesan.com

SAMPLE COLOR PALETTES

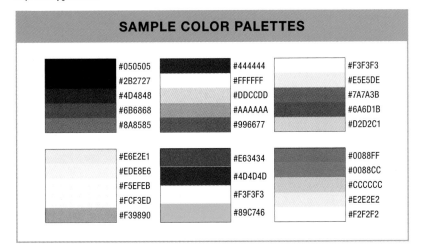

	#050505
	#2B2727
	#4D4848
	#6B6868
	#8A8585

	#444444
	#FFFFFF
	#DDCCDD
	#AAAAAA
	#996677

	#F3F3F3
	#E5E5DE
	#7A7A3B
	#6A6D1B
	#D2D2C1

	#E6E2E1
	#EDE8E6
	#F5EFEB
	#FCF3ED
	#F39890

	#E63434
	#4D4D4D
	#F3F3F3
	#89C746

	#0088FF
	#0088CC
	#CCCCCC
	#E2E2E2
	#F2F2F2

http://www.leakingmind.com

WHITE

White is an underrated—and often over-looked—color option. The restraint that is required to use white space heavily, or to rely on the least attention-grabbing color option, is no doubt tough. However, as with many challenging approaches, the result of such restraint can be spectacular and well worth the effort. The following sites use ample white space. This lends them a light and airy feel, making them uncongested and easy on the eyes. The use of white often borders on minimalism, but that doesn't have to be the case. Most of these sites have extensive, non-minimal designs.

Take the Coudal Partners site, for example. This is an unpretentious site. Its beautiful design was created with simplicity and lots of white space. It would have been easy to clutter this site with complex visual elements. The strong use of typography greatly enhances the design, but white sets the mood. Its clean, professional, high-end connotations present the company in a positive light. The heavy use of white reflects the company's refined style that relies on effective design rather than design trends.

It should be noted that white does not equal boring. Take the Vectorian site, for example. This simple-looking site is loaded with style. Instead of emphasizing the content's frame, it focuses on the content itself. Yet the design has enough life to make it distinct and memorable. There are many complex designs that are far more forgettable than this beautiful site.

It seems that this is probably one of the styles that seldom gets considered. A super clean, colorless design certainly doesn't sound exciting, and such an approach may make for a difficult pitch. Not many clients will be enticed by the idea of a clean design that doesn't attempt to pound its message into the viewer's mind. Nonetheless, these designs prove that just such an approach has many attractive qualities that make it a viable option worth pursuing and promoting.

Connotations of white: pure, stable, trustworthy, happy, clean, fresh. Also associated with life, goodness, marriage, peace, winter and cold.

http://coudal.com

http://www.mindfour.com

http://www.mstefan.com/blog

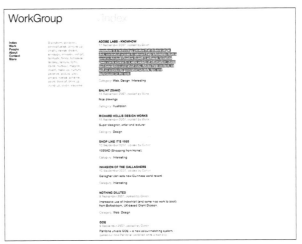

http://www.vectorian.de

http://www.workgroup.ie

http://www.limedesign.co.nz

http://www.bbdata.ca

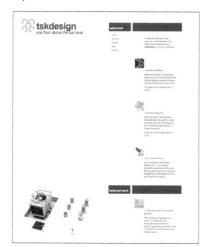

http://www.tskdesign.ro

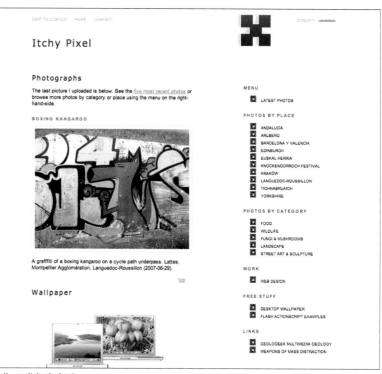

http://www.itchypixel.net

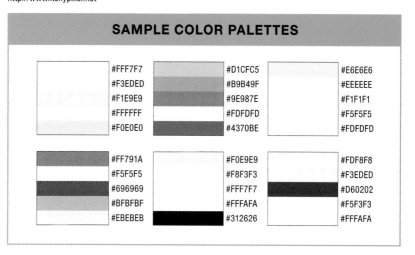

SAMPLE COLOR PALETTES

	#FFF7F7		#D1CFC5		#E6E6E6		
	#F3EDED		#B9B49F		#EEEEEE		
	#F1E9E9		#9E987E		#F1F1F1		
	#FFFFFF		#FDFDFD		#F5F5F5		
	#F0E0E0		#4370BE		#FDFDFD		
	#FF791A		#F0E9E9		#FDF8F8		
	#F5F5F5		#F8F3F3		#F3EDED		
	#696969		#FFF7F7		#D60202		
	#BFBFBF		#FFFAFA		#F5F3F3		
	#EBEBEB		#312626		#FFFAFA		

BLACK & WHITE

Most of the sites in this chapter could have gone into either the black or the white category, but their nearly pure black-and-white nature is strikingly distinct and merits a category all its own. One can't help but ponder a connection between the simple beauty of these sites and the appeal of black-and-white photography. The aesthetic of this traditional photography method applies remarkably well to these sites, and many of its connotations translate into this digital medium.

Perhaps the biggest irony of the black-and-white sites is this: It seems as though instinct would dictate that black-and-white sites would be less noticeable and more easily ignored, but this could not be more incorrect. In fact, black-and-white sites can be eye candy, and the contrast of the two colors forces the content to leap off the page toward the viewer. Additionally, when color is introduced into these otherwise stark palettes, it becomes even more effective.

The portfolio site of Julien Eichinger is a superb example of the power a black-and-white design can have. In this case, the ornate, classy design is further elevated by the use of a matching, and equally classy, color palette. The black-and-white combo plays into the site's overall aesthetic and was an excellent choice. Consider if the black had been some hot color like pink or orange; the entire message conveyed in the design would have changed. Instead, this site is beautifully executed and feels wonderfully refined.

http://justice.anglican.org.nz

http://perso.orange.fr/pixeldragon/portfolio5

http://www.clearwired.com

http://www.frzi.com

http://www.digitalwellbeing.eu/dwb

http://www.cocoatech.com

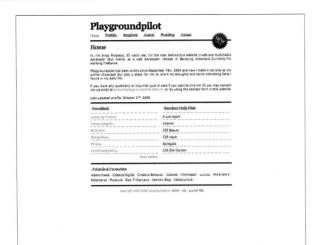

http://www.playgroundpilot.com

http://www.pauljohns.com

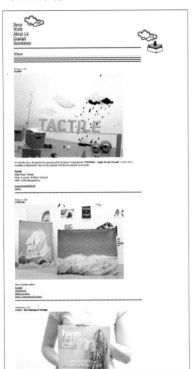

http://www.pixelgarten.de

http://www.m1k3.net

http://www.hyperisland.se

154

http://www.onebyone.com.au

http://www.peterpixel.nl

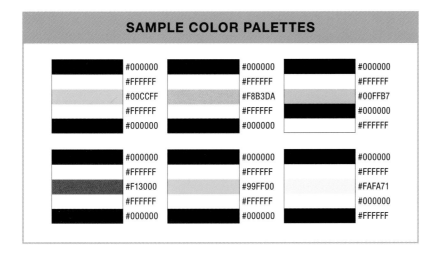

SAMPLE COLOR PALETTES

#000000	#000000	#000000
#FFFFFF	#FFFFFF	#FFFFFF
#00CCFF	#F8B3DA	#00FFB7
#FFFFFF	#FFFFFF	#000000
#000000	#000000	#FFFFFF

#000000	#000000	#000000
#FFFFFF	#FFFFFF	#FFFFFF
#F13000	#99FF00	#FAFA71
#FFFFFF	#FFFFFF	#000000
#000000	#000000	#FFFFFF

PINK & BLUE

The most remarkable thing about the pink-and-blue combo is how it defies the stereotypes typically associated with the pair. The first thing that comes to mind with this palette is boys, girls and babies, yet none of the samples in this chapter have anything to do with these topics.

The Pulp Cards site, for example, has used the combo to create a fun and playful atmosphere. I particularly like how they used pink to highlight key elements that they don't want you to miss, while the blue plays a more supportive role. This makes good sense, considering that pink tends to attract more attention than blue.

Another site that shows how the combo can be found in some interesting places is the Greatestcase site. This site is dedicated to handy snippets of PHP code. I can't say that I know many programmers who would find the use of pink and blue appealing, much less implement it in such an effective way. In this case, the color combo puts a fresh spin on otherwise bland content. Let's face it, code isn't exactly a great design element. Thus, a fun color palette applied to the code in a unique way creates a very distinct style, and it enables the content to contribute to the overall beauty of the design. Amazingly, this

site has almost made the code a small work of art, and programmers are keen on considering their code works of art.

For a third example that shows the color set in an unexpected location, take a look at the MindMeister site. The use of pink and blue in this case defies the technical-minded assumptions not only of software, but also of this particular type of software. The color combo sets a fun and attractive mood for the site that entices visitors with the expectation that this truly is a unique product. (And it is a rather impressive web application that is worth checking out.)

http://www.blond-kassel.de

http://www.pulpcards.co.uk

http://www.mindmeister.com

http://gtc.td-webdesign.se

http://www.atomplastic.com

http://www.teaandcrumpets.org

http://www.fakefrench.com

http://www.pinksandblues.com

http://www.puccipetwear.com

SAMPLE COLOR PALETTES

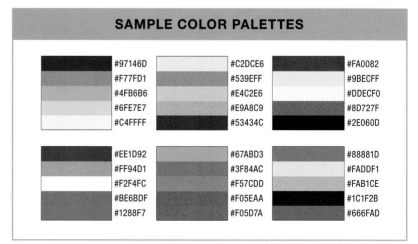

#97146D	#C2DCE6	#FA0082
#F77FD1	#539EFF	#9BECFF
#4FB6B6	#E4C2E6	#DDECF0
#6FE7E7	#E9A8C9	#8D727F
#C4FFFF	#53434C	#2E060D

#EE1D92	#67ABD3	#88881D
#FF94D1	#3F84AC	#FADDF1
#F2F4FC	#F57CDD	#FAB1CE
#BE6BDF	#F05EAA	#1C1F2B
#1288F7	#F05D7A	#666FAD

158

BLUE & GREEN

The blue-and-green combo is a trusty standby that has been called upon countless times to create what is easily one of the most conservative and attractive color combinations. It always looks great and is safe, but this doesn't mean that the blue-and-green choice is necessarily boring. The samples provided here are far from boring, but rather are vibrant and alive. Perhaps that is just what is intended. These colors of nature connect with everything that is life-giving. Green suggests plants and growth, while blue conjures thoughts of air and water.

Consider some alternative choices like green and brown or blue and brown, both of which allude to nature. These combinations have completely differ-

ent connotations and certainly give an entirely different meaning to sites using them. Blue and brown together often comes off as hip and trendy (though this will likely change over time). Meanwhile, the green-and-brown combo has a dirty, plantlike feel to it. Blue and green somehow seem to be the most connected to a universal "natural" connotation. It is amazing to see how color choice changes the entire feel of a site.

So how is it that such a "natural" combination of colors is often found on sites for such "unnatural" products as software? Well, these sites want to draw on the friendly, natural feel of the colors and convince potential clients that the application is easy to use. Sure,

this is a subtle connection, but in design every element matters, and every element adds up to the cumulative effect of the design. So, if a design is easy on the eyes and feels friendly, this says something about the product behind the design. Want your widget to look friendly? Dress it in friendly colors.

Many sites feature what might be considered "micro services" because they meet a very specific set of niche needs. This is exactly the case with The Choppr. This may be a lighthearted site, but it is selling a service. The main reason users would be interested in using this service is if it offers them a skill they don't already have, so making it feel like an easy process is absolutely key.

http://thechoppr.com

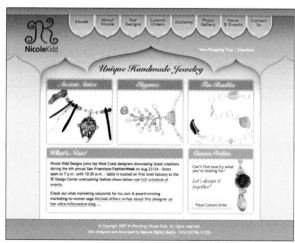

http://www.nicolekidd.com

http://www.watertankco.com.au

http://www.tweakcast.com

http://www.hellomedia.com.au

http://iconkits.com

http://www.hbcweb.com

http://www.creixems.com/eng

http://www.flippingpad.com

http://www.professionalontheweb.com

http://www.uncover.com

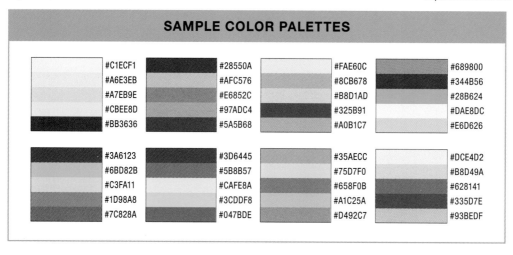

SAMPLE COLOR PALETTES

#C1ECF1	#28550A	#FAE60C	#689800
#A6E3EB	#AFC576	#8CB678	#344B56
#A7EB9E	#E6852C	#B8D1AD	#28B624
#CBEE8D	#97ADC4	#325B91	#DAE8DC
#BB3636	#5A5B68	#A0B1C7	#E6D626
#3A6123	#3D6445	#35AECC	#DCE4D2
#6BD82B	#5B8B57	#75D7F0	#B8D49A
#C3FA11	#CAFE8A	#658F0B	#628141
#1D98A8	#3CDDF8	#A1C25A	#335D7E
#7C828A	#047BDE	#D492C7	#93BEDF

BOLD

This grouping of sites makes use of bold colors that pop out of the page. These web designs are saturated with rich colors that create an intense aesthetic. This approach is used for an assortment of reasons, but one thing is always true: Bold colors such as these always produce a lively and active atmosphere.

Bold color use embraces computer technology and disregards the color limitations of print. These intense colors are unique to the digital world because they cannot be achieved easily in printed mediums. This has the wonderful benefit of allowing web designers to use colors that have been avoided for decades.

One of the more successful examples of this is the AM Design site. Not only does the site have an intense background color, but it also has the same color style worked into all the photographs in the content section. This elevates the style from trendy to holistic, since the entire design is unified by this common approach. This site is distinct and leaves a lasting impression. It is amazing how much this design firm stands out just by basing its site presentation on color use—as opposed to more conservative approaches. The color drives the site's message, and this is further emphasized through its funny, almost ironic, photography.

Another example of effective bold color usage is the Carbonmade site. This site offers a service to artists, which enables them to build online portfolios with ease. The bold colors do two things for the site. First, they make it look easy and fun to use. Creative types are not necessarily interested in figuring out the nuances of a new service. By designing the site with a fun color scheme, users are encouraged to sign up for its service. The playful imagery works to this end as well. Secondly, the strong colors make the site stand out, making it lively and enjoyable to look at.

http://www.amdesign.com

http://www.carbonmade.com

http://www.danielpospisil.cz

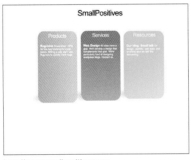

http://www.smallpositives.com

http://www.nterface.com

http://www.swaroopch.com

http://wp-themes.designdisease.com

http://www.sitemost.com.au

http://www.stargraphicdesign.com

http://www.citricox.com

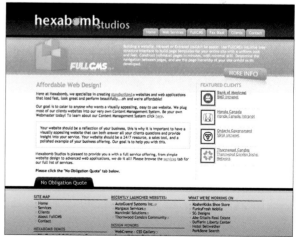

http://www.hexabomb.com

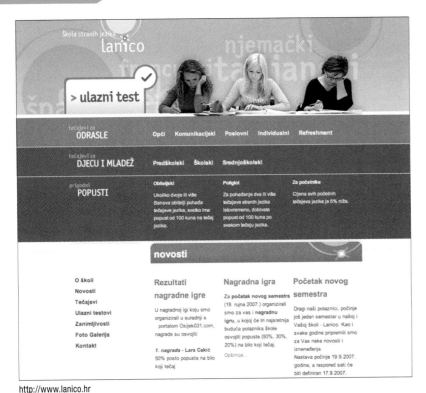

http://www.lanico.hr

http://www.939design.com

SAMPLE COLOR PALETTES

#FC0082	#00EEBB	#108CA5	#F8E02B	#63F71E	
#FF2B98	#BBFE18	#0E6B7E	#F04848	#DDF71E	
#FFC9E5	#FDA307	#14C7EB	#C86BEC	#161616	
#77C90D	#FF0051	#8CEB14	#30C0F0	#F7291D	
#F5FFAD	#160C0D	#EB1459	#52D352	#FF3680	

#DDB001	#AAE447	#FF3709	#FFFFFF	#47E9FF	
#00B9F0	#D3DA14	#FDFED2	#FC4AA0	#7AFD2E	
#FC11B9	#ECF1E3	#A4D933	#FCD84A	#F8630F	
#F07967	#102210	#3BB512	#000000	#F756FD	
#E3E014	#F31D7A	#102006	#4AE6FC	#FFFF47	

MUTED

The muted color palette is essentially the polar opposite of the bold approach. Instead of working to make everything aggressive and in-your-face, muted palettes are restrained and often sophisticated. Their reservation presents a more controlled attitude and can be very relaxing and refreshing amid the popular use of saturated colors.

One major bonus of working with such a palette is that when something needs to stand out, it can be made to do so very easily. Simply add a bit of full saturated color and suddenly the element is bursting off the page. Of course, too much of this can destroy the atmosphere created by a muted color scheme

and reduce other elements' ability to pop. Still, it is a powerful feature of this style. Actually, this isn't just a bonus, but perhaps the real reason to use this type of palette. Take a look at Lucky Oliver, for example. The site sells stock photography, so a muted palette is a logical choice. The design is stylish and impressive, but what is truly admirable is that it doesn't interfere with the content. This is quite an achievement, considering the rich detail in the design. I largely credit the muted palette for this feat. The sample photographs jump off the page and sell themselves. It is refreshing to see that the muted palette does not inherently create a boring design.

Sometimes a muted palette isn't necessarily used to make other elements pop but is rather used to establish mood. Such is the case with Aarron Walter's site. It is entirely built on muted colors, and no elements are given sharp contrast. In this case the designer has created a refined and restrained atmosphere. I don't know Aarron, but his site leads me to suspect that he is a smart guy who is good at his job but who lacks the pretension commonly associated with highbrow design. His muted palette communicates a message about who he is. As you can see, the effects of color selection are profound even if they work on a subconscious level.

http://www.luckyoliver.com

http://aarronwalter.com

http://styleboost.com

http://www.survivingthepixel.com

http://www.mostpreviewed.com

http://www.jamiegregory.co.uk

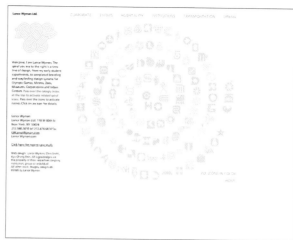

http://www.lancewyman.com

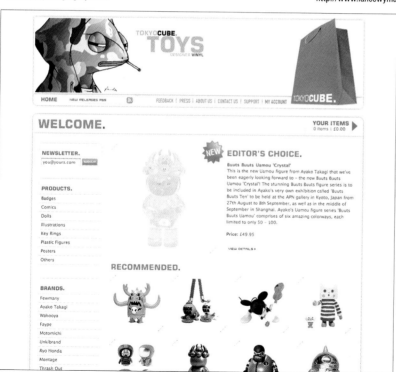

http://shop.tokyocube.com

http://www.antilimit.com

http://www.frosk.org

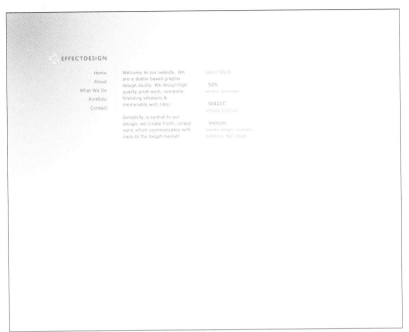

http://www.effect.ie

http://www.serph.com

http://www.nypocreative.co.uk

SAMPLE COLOR PALETTES

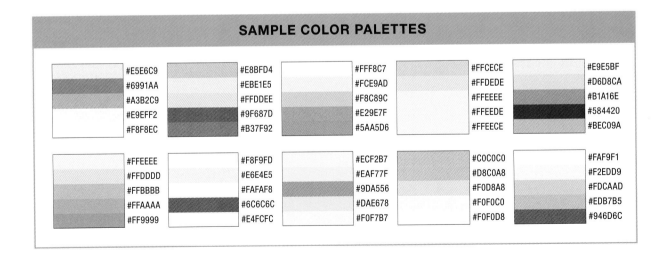

#E5E6C9	#E8BFD4
#6991AA	#EBE1E5
#A3B2C9	#FFDDEE
#E9EFF2	#9F687D
#F8F8EC	#B37F92

#FFF8C7	#FFCECE
#FCE9AD	#FFDEDE
#F8C89C	#FFEEEE
#E29E7F	#FFEEDE
#5AA5D6	#FFEECE

#E9E5BF	
#D6D8CA	
#B1A16E	
#584420	
#BEC09A	

#FFEEEE	#F8F9FD
#FFDDDD	#E6E4E5
#FFBBBB	#FAFAF8
#FFAAAA	#6C6C6C
#FF9999	#E4FCFC

#ECF2B7	#C0C0C0
#EAF77F	#D8C0A8
#9DA556	#F0D8A8
#DAE678	#F0F0C0
#F0F7B7	#F0F0D8

#FAF9F1	
#F2EDD9	
#FDCAAD	
#EDB7B5	
#946D6C	

05

Icons Dates & Calendars Rounded Corners Folded Corners Rays Tags Crests Badges Stripes Ornate Elements Ornate Backgrounds Gradients Shine

SITES BY ELEMENT

Design elements come in a wide array of shapes, sizes and styles. Some reflect trendy approaches (badges, for example), while others result from pure necessity. What is truly fascinating about these groupings, though, is that each and every one has a purpose. Each has a way of being used that elevates it from randomness to clear purpose. Yet each of these elements can be wasted and reduced to a worthless role when used without intent. Even worse, when neglected, these design elements actually detract from the overall site design. Consider the ineffective styling of a calendar control, a small, seemingly insignificant element that tends to look rather bland in its default skin. The lesson here is that as designers we must consider every item we use in a design. Whether they are functional or decorative, all the elements of a design must be unified by an overall aesthetic.

05

SITES BY ELEMENT

Icons Dates & Calendars Rounded Corners Folded Corners Rays Tags Crests Badges Stripes Ornate Elements Ornate Backgrounds Gradients Shine

ICONS

Icons are incredible little visual devices. Their sole purpose is to communicate lots of information in the simplest possible way. Their use on the web is no surprise. The web is an environment filled with impatience, wandering eyes and easy distractions. It is a place in dire need of quick visual indicators. Icons can serve as great helpers that show us where to go for what we need. Instead of scanning text you can scan images, and often they will tell you what you need. This is no different than a street sign that uses recognizable forms to communicate quicker than text.

The Elixir Graphics homepage is a terrific demonstration of the power of icons. It is no surprise that the site uses icons, because it sells them. All the same, the prominence on the homepage is quite powerful. Each of the three main icons connects perfectly with the content that lies beneath. The text below each icon spells it out, but the graphics remain impressed upon the visitor's mind. This surprisingly simple homepage is loaded with style and has a very distinct feel.

Another good reason to put icons to work is to do the exact opposite of the Elixir Graphics site. In some cases, icons can be used to cut through the visual clutter to help guide visitors to the content they are most interested in. Such is the case with E-junkie. The homepage for this site is heavy with content, which enables visitors to get the gist of the site's services quickly without having to look too far. This does run the risk of overwhelming the user, though. Icons have been put to work to mitigate this problem. Here, nice large icons have been used to identify the buckets of data down the side, allowing users to scan for the topic they are most concerned about.

A common problem for designers is that icons can feel out of place. There are two key elements to consider when placing icons into a design. First, they should fit the color scheme of the site. This might mean customizing a stock set of icons or hand-building brand new ones. Second, the icons must fit with the style of the site. If the site is bubbly and shiny, the icons should be as well. A perfect matching of style and color has been achieved on Indian Geeks. The square shape of the icons is reflected in the various square-cornered boxes in the page. And the white, almost luminous color of the icons is again reflected in the overall color of the site.

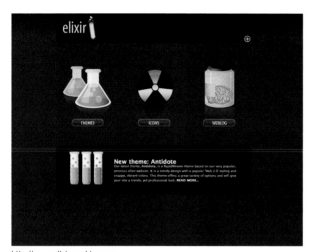

http://www.elixirgraphics.com

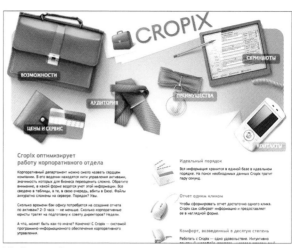

http://www.cropix.ru

http://www.e-junkie.com

http://www.ripple.org

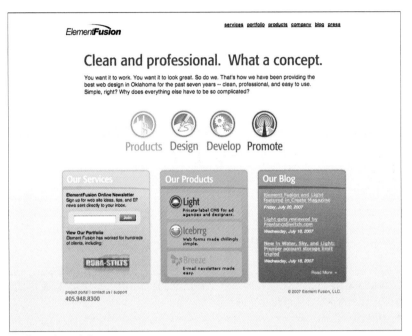

http://www.elementfusion.com

http://www.igeeks.org

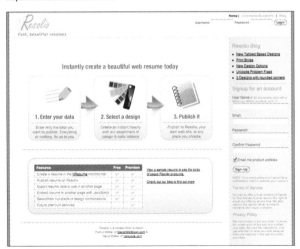

http://resolio.com

http://www.splitdivision.com

05

SITES BY ELEMENT

Icons   Dates & Calendars   Rounded Corners   Folded Corners   Rays   Tags   Crests   Badges   Stripes   Ornate Elements   Ornate Backgrounds   Gradients   Shine

DATES & CALENDARS

Attention to detail is one of the most important traits of a successful designer. Following through on the final details of a site's design can transform it from something OK into something great. Believe it or not, some slick styling on an element as simple as the date stamp on a blog post or a nice clean calendar design can really add a lot of life to a site. This is an additional way to establish and unify a design. The date could be a boring string of text; instead, these sites have turned it into a beautiful aspect of their design.

Transforming the date element into a design flourish is exactly what has been done on the Kev Adamson site. The dates on the site have been styled to look like a spiral-bound calendar. Not only does the style fit the sketchy style of the site, but it also reinforces the information visually.

Another reason to style dates in some special way is to draw attention to them. Before doing so, first consider the importance of dates in your hierarchy and design. Then style them appropriately to get the needed emphasis for the hierarchy you want. A fine demonstration of this can be found on the Riverfront Park site. The date display on this site has a nice decorative touch, which makes it a bit more prominent. Of course, the date of a post is not the most important element, so while it does highlight the date, it by no means becomes the main focus.

In contrast to making the date stand out, the Nclud site has styled the calendar so it blends perfectly with the site. It matches the background and stays out of the way. The goal is to allow for the functionality without attracting attention—and a poorly designed calendar would quickly stick out.

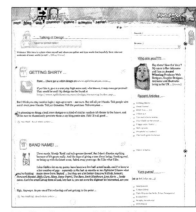

http://kevadamson.com/talking-of-design

http://www.nclud.com/sketchbook

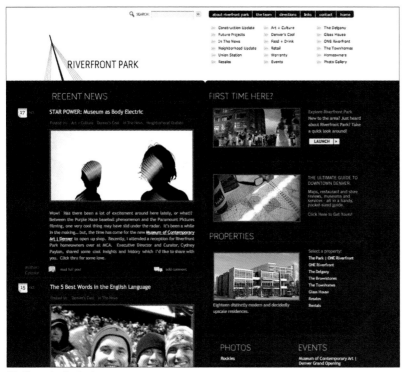

http://www.riverfrontpark.com

http://www.avenuegc.co.uk

http://alexsancho.name

http://www.squible.com

http://www.anderswahlberg.com/blogg

http://www.newearthonline.co.uk

05

SITES BY ELEMENT

Icons · Dates & Calendars · **Rounded Corners** · Folded Corners · Rays · Tags · Crests · Badges · Stripes · Ornate Elements · Ornate Backgrounds · Gradients · Shine

ROUNDED CORNERS

The rounded corner has been a mainstay in web design since the beginning of the Internet. Designers often use rounded corners for random, illogical reasons, but all elements have their place. The trick is to figure out what that place is. At the heart of any design element lies a message to be communicated to the user. Even something as simple as rounded corners will connect with the viewer in some way, no matter how subtly.

Rounded corners are used most logically when they fit the style of the site in some obvious way. Take the Scott Saw site, for example. Here, the rounded corners match the organic artwork.

The secondary purpose of rounded corners is to break up the boxlike nature of web design. With rounded cor-ners, we are not confined to table-like layouts, as we can interlock rounded shapes that invoke a visual unification of the design. Do not underestimate the power of rounded corners. A site that has successfully taken this approach is Mobaito. The repetition of rounded corners unifies the design, and the entire site becomes a single massive entity. The issue for the Mobaito site is figuring out how the style plays into the ideas of the site. In other words, is this still poor use of rounded corners due to lack of purpose? Visually speaking, the unification of the page is extremely valuable. Plus, soft rounded corners on a career site make job hunting less daunting. This is a subtle message, but it is ever-present.

http://www.scottsaw.com

http://www.us.mobaito.com

http://www.2440media.com

http://www.dtelepathy.com

http://www.scriggleit.com

http://lifelike.se

http://www.leandaryan.com

05
SITES BY ELEMENT

Icons Dates & Calendars Rounded Corners **Folded Corners** Rays Tags Crests Badges Stripes Ornate Elements Ornate Backgrounds Gradients Shine

FOLDED CORNERS

The folded corner is a simple design element that attempts to give the page (or some element in the page) the appearance of being curled up or folded over. At the most basic level this serves to associate the page with the printed form. Many times online material can be considered unreliable, and associating the online material with the "real" thing can make the content seem more trustworthy. It is also possible that the subject matter itself may relate to the printed form.

Regardless of the purpose, there are countless ways to use this simple element. For an example of the literal use, take a look at the Ungarbage site, which talks about recycling on the web. These are, of course, web "pages" that are being recycled; the folded page corners allude to physical paper. These folded corners play into the site's theme and support its overall purpose.

In other cases, the folded corner is used as a dramatic and eye-catching visual element. Miingle, for example, has a massive curled page effect. The element dominates the page and demands visitors' attention. In this way the folded page highlights the main action the visitors are supposed to take—booking an ad campaign.

Finally, the element can be used for purely aesthetic reasons. Such is the case with Webstruments. Here we find a page curl that only serves to enhance the look of the page. There is nothing inherently wrong with this. The key is to make the element fit in, and in this case the page curl fits in wonderfully and contributes to the slick design.

http://www.ungarbage.com

http://www.mattinglydesign.net

179

http://webstruments.com

http://www.mrwebhead.com

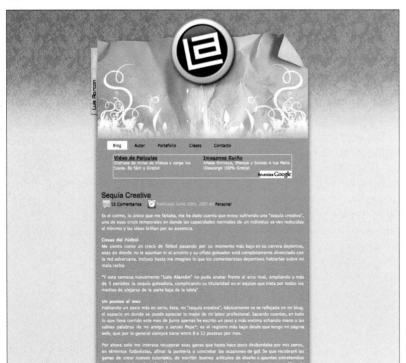

http://www.luisalarcon.com/blog

http://www.teresawalsh.com

http://www.silverorange.com

05

SITES BY ELEMENT

Icons Dates & Calendars Rounded Corners Folded Corners **Rays** Tags Crests Badges Stripes Ornate Elements Ornate Backgrounds Gradients Shine

RAYS

The ray can be a subtle part of a page's design, employed to emphasize the logo or another key element. On the other hand, it can create the entire mood of a site, adding motion to an otherwise static design.

On the Royale Vibes site we find simple yet beautiful ray use. The radial pattern adds depth to the header and almost seems to be pointing to the site's title. It breathes life into this part of the page by giving it a sense of action. It is also a very noticeable element, which moves it up in the hierarchy of the page. This helps to reinforce the brand of the site and to remind visitors what site they are reading. Overall, this makes for a very powerful page header.

Another site that has used the element in a wonderful way is Guilago. In this case the ray is again used to add motion, but this time it reinforces the motion already established by the large illustrated figure. Additionally, the ray supports the semi-retro theme of the site.

The ray design element can also be playful and fun. Take a look at the DJ Timbo site, for example. The site is selling a service, but it presents that service in a humorous way. The radial design in the background helps establish this over-the-top style and makes the experience of exploring the site more visually entertaining.

http://royalevibes.com

http://guilago.se

http://www.elan3.com

http://www.djtimbo.com

http://www.bio-bak.nl

182

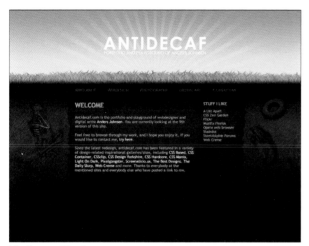

http://www.antidecaf.com

http://incrediblebox.com

http://www.samcreate.com/blog

http://fluxility.com

http://www.interestingfacts.org

05

SITES BY ELEMENT

Icons Dates & Calendars Rounded Corners Folded Corners Rays **Tags** Crests Badges Stripes Ornate Elements Ornate Backgrounds Gradients Shine

TAGS

The use of tags (as in hanging price tags) is another minor pattern in web design. Perhaps this chapter is just the result of way too much web browsing. Then again, here is a nice collection of sites that have made use of this element. Whatever the case, there is at least a handful of sites that have used this element remarkably well. Essentially, tags serve the same purpose as elements like badges or radial patterns. While those elements are bold, the tag is subtle in the way it draws attention to a certain element. In many of these designs it is the angled nature of the tag that draws the attention. It is pretty remarkable that simply tilting the tag can give it such emphasis in a design.

A perfect demonstration of this style is the SimoneStudio site. The company's name and a two-word mission statement have been placed inside a decorative tag, which is situated so it sits at an angle and crosses the borders of the header. It is the focus of the page and quickly draws attention. This guarantees that visitors catch the name of the firm and the style of work they do. As with any well-polished site, the tag doesn't feel out of place. The entire page has been considered, so the design works as a whole. Plus, the company designs fabrics, so using a tag fits the type of work they do, making the use of this element even more natural.

Sometimes a design element like this can be a simple flourish on a site, and other times the same element can become the defining factor for an entire site. This defining factor approach is what we find on Big Sweater Design. This site turns the idea of a clothing tag into a full theme. It is amazing how a design is transformed when it uses a theme such as this. The entire process becomes more fun, and visitors become even more intrigued by the site. It turns a standard site into an experience and greatly increases its chances of being remembered.

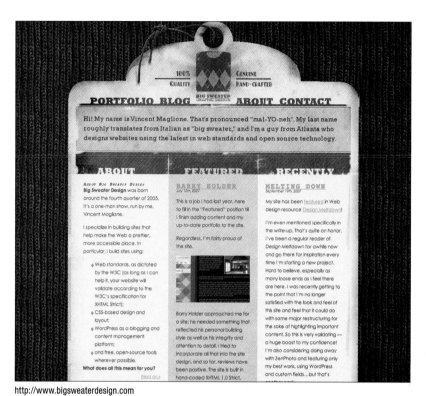

http://www.bigsweaterdesign.com

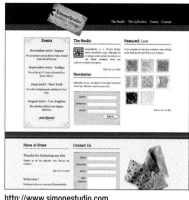

http://www.simonestudio.com

http://www.rebeccapaterson.co.uk

http://www.gospodicna.si

http://www.flyingturtle.net

185

http://www.okb.es

http://www.outline2design.com

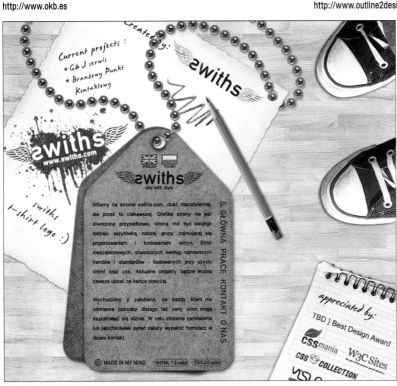

http://www.swiths.com

05
SITES BY ELEMENT

Icons Dates & Calendars Rounded Corners Folded Corners Rays Tags Crests Badges Stripes Ornate Elements Ornate Backgrounds Gradients Shine

CRESTS

Historically, crests have been reserved for kings and queens. They stood as symbols of alignment. But today anything goes, and consequently the crest can be found in many forms—often as a decorative, meaningless symbol. The crest can act as an eye-catching element to communicate important information to the viewer. It has a certain power in this regard and can be a useful tool when used effectively.

A terrific example of practical use of the crest is the Golf Medic site. The name alone brings up serious, medical-related imagery. When combined with the perceived class of golf, the resulting custom crest alludes to both the medical connotations and the golf theme. In this case the crest not only serves as the focal point for the logo, but it also becomes the most thematic and mood-setting element of the design. It establishes a professional and serious atmosphere while communicating the primary subject matter of the site. A design element that multitasks is always a good thing and is a sure sign of thoughtful and effective design.

In other designs, much more entertaining uses of the crest can be found. Such is the case of the Small Farm Design site. Here the crest sets the mood, but it is far from serious. The crest is made into a silly egg and rooster design, and although it is aesthetically pleasing, it speaks volumes about the people behind this design studio and conjures expectations of a fun, easygoing staff.

One of the most exciting uses of the crest is for establishing a cool, hip, designer feel. A fine sample of this is the Waetzig Design site. The crest in this design is merged wonderfully into the site's concept and layout, yet it is not used in such a way as to become the focal point of the page. Instead, it is just an element added to the page to help reinforce its overall beauty.

http://www.smallfarmdesign.com

http://www.waetzigdesign.com

http://www.alexswanson.net/blog

http://www.golfmedic.net

http://www.joinradius.com

http://www.factioninc.com

http://contrabrand.net

http://www.djdynamike.com

http://www.loicsans.com

http://pixelfly.net

SAMPLE COLOR PALETTES

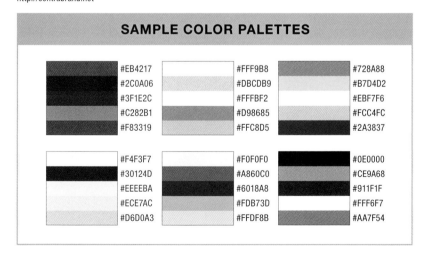

	#EB4217
	#2C0A06
	#3F1E2C
	#C282B1
	#F83319

	#FFF9B8
	#DBCDB9
	#FFFBF2
	#D98685
	#FFC8D5

	#728A88
	#B7D4D2
	#EBF7F6
	#FCC4FC
	#2A3837

	#F4F3F7
	#30124D
	#EEEEBA
	#ECE7AC
	#D6D0A3

	#F0F0F0
	#A860C0
	#6018A8
	#FDB73D
	#FFDF8B

	#0E0000
	#CE9A68
	#911F1F
	#FFF6F7
	#AA7F54

05

SITES BY ELEMENT

Icons Dates & Calendars Rounded Corners Folded Corners Rays Tags Crests **Badges** Stripes Ornate Elements Ornate Backgrounds Gradients Shine

BADGES

A badge is a design element that is often perceived as frivolous. As it turns out, these little dudes have a job, and they do it exceedingly well. These suckers are intended to be attention-grabbers that communicate key pieces of information. This is pretty much their only purpose in life. The value of the information they contain varies. Typically, the information either encourages users to take some desired step, or it is a link to the key action item that the site owners want the visitor to take.

A fine example to start with is the Simon Wiffen site. The simple "Download songs here" badge serves as an attention-grabbing call-to-action. As a music-oriented site, it is crucial that they get potential customers to listen to and enjoy the music. A nice visually prominent badge does a fine job of drawing attention to a key step for the site.

The Plushie Corner site makes interesting use of badges. Here, the main navigation is actually contained within individual badges. This is a unique approach to navigation and manages to effectively draw attention to this key element of the page. The color of the badges is also interesting since badges are often visually reinforced through high-contrast colors. Instead, subtle colors have been used, and the badges more effectively blend with the site.

The important thing to keep in mind when using this element is that it inevitably draws a lot of attention. As such, it is wise to use it to communicate something of importance. Putting meaningless content in a badge is a waste of valuable space in what could be the most visually dominating element of the design.

http://www.simonwiffen.co.uk

http://www.jasonlarosedesign.com

http://www.saturdate.org

http://www.brandempire.com

http://plushie.avocadolite.com

http://www.merix.com.pl

http://www.dolphincruises.co.nz

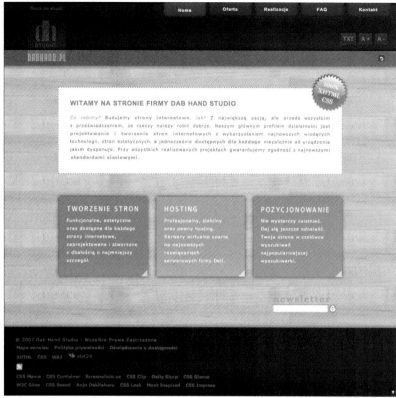

http://www.dabhand.pl

http://www.webleeddesign.com

05
SITES BY ELEMENT

Icons Dates & Calendars Rounded Corners Folded Corners Rays Tags Crests Badges **Stripes** Ornate Elements Ornate Backgrounds Gradients Shine

STRIPES

This simple element is such a minimal part of a design that it almost feels silly to dedicate a whole chapter to it. Nevertheless, stripes are used heavily and merit some discussion. As minimal as the element may be, I don't want to trivialize any of the designs included in this chapter, because they are outstanding. Categorizing these sites based on one small element of their design might seem brutal, but I think their categorization serves to show how the element can enhance a site in a thoughtful and beautiful way.

One wonderful example is the First-flash site. Here we find large and bold stripes as a decorative background element. Stripes are most commonly used in backgrounds. I selected this site as an example because it offers a variation on the simpler, evenly striped pattern. The variety in the background adds visual depth to this site. The stripes have been unified with the design through the use of color. Notice how the colors of the main links match the background. Unification is a key principle with the stripe element, as it keeps the stripes from feeling out of place; they simply must be connected to the overall design.

http://www.firstflash.net

http://www.michaelcourier.com

http://www.notcot.org

http://www.copious.co.uk

http://www.errolschwartz.com

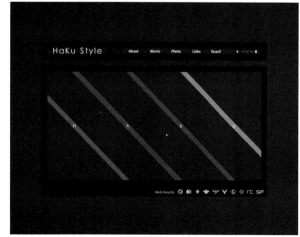

http://www.hakustyle.com

http://www.bouroullec.com

http://www.distancemedia.co.uk

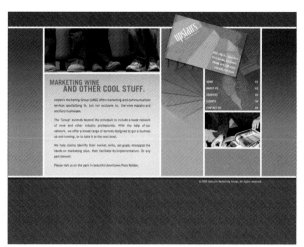

http://www.upstairsmarketing.com

http://www.casperelectronics.com

http://run.likethewind.ca

05
SITES BY ELEMENT

Icons Dates & Calendars Rounded Corners Folded Corners Rays Tags Crests Badges Stripes Ornate Elements Ornate Backgrounds Gradients Shine

ORNATE ELEMENTS

Ornate elements may gain trendy status from time to time, but on the whole they will never go away or be out of style. Ornament has always been beautiful, and its popularity extends far into the past, well before the Internet. What is truly wonderful is that web designers still find ways to use ornament in fresh, new and beautiful ways—not just beautiful in a Victorian, old-school sort of way, but in a modern, stylish way.

A gorgeous example of effectively used ornament is DigitalKick. This site could have easily fallen into the old-fashioned corner. Instead, it has a classy, modern style. The combination of delicate ornament and pixel-based details deflects the old-fashioned aesthetic. This is significant because it shows the style's diversity. Ornament is perhaps one of the most flexible design styles available. The style's effect depends on the type of ornate element and the connotations it carries. Part of the DigitalKick site's magic is that a classic design ornament was merged with modern elements of pixel-based design. Throw in some classic imagery and you have a cool hodgepodge of design styles. This is a difficult balance to maintain, but the DigitalKick site has achieved it admirably.

Another site that gives a whole new feel to the element is the Brainfood site. This site is a joy to look at and puts a fresh spin on ornament use. There are two contributors to this fresh feel: the atypical color palette and the modern glossiness. The power of the ornament is revealed when it is morphed into something special, beautiful and distinct, like it is on the Brainfood site.

http://www.digitalkick.com

http://www.brainfood.com

http://www.berenguer.info

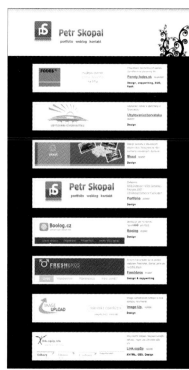

http://www.fishbond.net

http://www.alexanderwalter.com

http://www.amberbowe.com

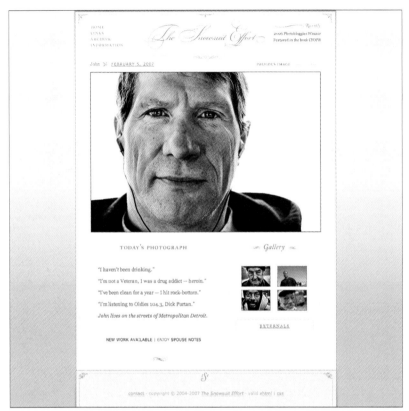

http://www.snowsuit.net

http://www.cabanadigital.com

http://www.matthew-design.com

05

SITES BY ELEMENT

Icons Dates & Calendars Rounded Corners Folded Corners Rays Tags Crests Badges Stripes Ornate Elements **Ornate Backgrounds** Gradients Shine

ORNATE BACKGROUNDS

Repeating ornate patterns have become a trend on the web. As with any trend, this one is often overdone and poorly used. But of course there will always be those sites that have used it so wonderfully that others are inspired to try the same. It is easy to misuse ornate patterns, so let's look at a few things to consider when incorporating it into a design.

The difference between success and failure in this case can be subtle. Ornate backgrounds can make a design feel crafty, classy, feminine, elegant or gritty. The potential connotations of the ornate element are extreme, but the one thing it universally indicates is style. Something about ornate patterns is just plain stylish. However, getting the ornate patterns to fit into the overall design is the primary concern.

The most fundamental thing to consider is making the color scheme work. Don't be afraid to edit that nice pattern and make the colors fit your purpose. A tight color scheme does wonders to enhance the quality of a site. The background should feel like a part of the design, not a separate unrelated element.

Be sure the connotations of the pattern match the overall theme of the site. An ornate background shouldn't be the first design choice but rather one of the last. After the desired feel has been established and the primary imagery has been selected, implement an ornate background only if it is a logical option.

Use ornament appropriately. An ornate background on a corporate information technology firm's website may be inappropriate. The same background on the website for an IT firm that installs wireless networks in high-class condos may be perfect. Consider the context and use the element fittingly.

http://photomatt.net

http://dailyminefield.com

http://www.cameronmoll.com

http://www.aftercode.com

http://www.hansthedouble.com

http://www.factory4.co.uk

http://www.24-7media.de

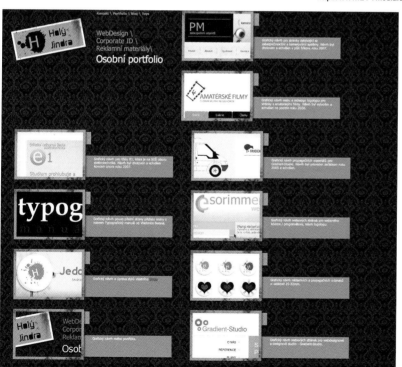

http://www.jindraholy.info

http://www.digitalemon.com

05

SITES BY ELEMENT

Icons   Dates & Calendars   Rounded Corners   Folded Corners   Rays   Tags   Crests   Badges   Stripes   Ornate Elements   Ornate Backgrounds   **Gradients**   Shine

GRADIENTS

Ah, the lovely gradient. This is another design element that can be found in nearly any design. This element is easily abused, but as these samples show, it can be beautifully used as well. The gradient is almost entirely about visual appeal. It carries very little meaning, and any meaning it does have typically comes from the way it is used or from the other elements it is mixed with. This is not to say that the gradient can't be used with deliberate purpose. You will see that this is often the case.

One thing all these sites share is a soft feel. They aren't hard-edged or rough. The ones with a gradient background have a misty vibe, which gives them a sort of light-emitting quality. I initially thought these gradients were arbitrary additions without a concept or big idea behind them. But now I think many of these sites are aiming for a soft, safe, comfortable feel, and they have employed strong use of gradients to accomplish this.

A prime example of this is the Pure Volume site. The abundance of gradients on this site certainly plays into its soft and mellow atmosphere, like a room dedicated to relaxing with good music. The soft, rounded corners of various site elements reinforce this effect.

The thing to remember is that no element or technique should be considered a quick or easy fix. Each element of a design should be thought through and planned. So if gradients such as these accomplish the goals of a site, feel free to use them.

This style is very flexible. Take a look at Nitram+Nunca, for example. The gradients here are subtle and soft, giving the site a warm feeling, especially when combined with the delicate browns. This strongly contrasts with Pioneer10, which uses the gradients in a more fashionable, almost techno sort of style. The gradient style is suitable for many situations, but finding situations where it stands out is the ultimate goal!

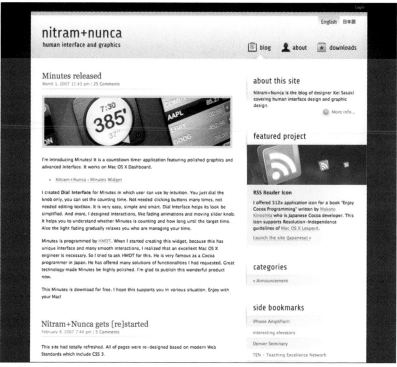

http://www.nitram-nunca.com

http://www.pioneer10.com

http://www.purevolume.com

http://www.hopkingdesign.com

http://www.kqed.org/quest

http://www.nonstop.tv/silver

http://www.lealea.net

http://payplay.fm

05
SITES BY ELEMENT

Icons Dates & Calendars Rounded Corners Folded Corners Rays Tags Crests Badges Stripes Ornate Elements Ornate Backgrounds Gradients **Shine**

SHINE

Adding shine or gloss to site elements is nothing new. Apple popularized the style long ago with its gel-like tabs, and it has been copied many thousands of times since. This style has slowly evolved over time. It has finally been formalized into a more refined approach in which the style is applied to sites thoroughly, instead of applying the shiny style to just a few elements. There are two key techniques required for mastery of this style.

High contrast with highly saturated colors. High contrast is required to create a glossy look. The best implementations of this style typically include highly saturated colors in conjunction with a large range of values. Consider a shiny new car. Would it look so polished if it was worn and the color muted with age? No, it wouldn't—and that's exactly why cars with a saturated color like red look so nice. The shine naturally shows up better on them. The same is true in the digital realm. Super-saturated colors combined with sharply contrasting whites look really polished.

The perfect demonstration of high contrast used to create the shiny style can be found on the CSStux site. The sharp contrast between pure black and white makes the site look polished. Even more fantastic is that the theme fits the site's brand. Think about the shiny shoes that come with a tux and the obvious connection between tuxedos and high-class design. This is a perfect match.

To see how to add saturated colors for a great application of this style, take a gander at the TalkXbox site, where you will see heavy use of black-and-white contrast. This site uses the shiny style not only to achieve a holistic, unified design but also to direct users' attention to key elements and action items.

Gradients galore. The second key element to the shiny site is the use of gradients. These are frequently seen as white overlays on objects that create the illusion of reflected light. But in the more complete samples, you can see how gradients have been used throughout in order to unify the design. Certain elements will have the super gloss, while supporting elements have more subtle gradients so they fit in well, even though they aren't as shiny.

A fine example of this can be found on the Defrost site. Its shiny style is less dramatic than previous samples, but most certainly it is being used. The gradients used throughout the rest of the design play into the idea of shine without themselves being shiny. In this way, these extra gradients unify the page and provide a supporting environment where the shiny tabs and buttons look great.

http://www.csstux.com

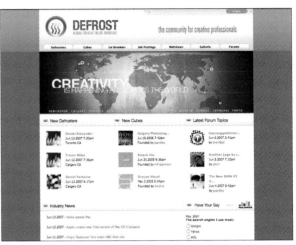

http://www.defrost.ca

http://arch-enemy.net

http://www.talkxbox.com

http://www.kloobik.org

http://www.egolounge.de

http://www.shape5.com

http://www.tamberlow.com

http://www.bkanal.ch

SAMPLE COLOR PALETTES

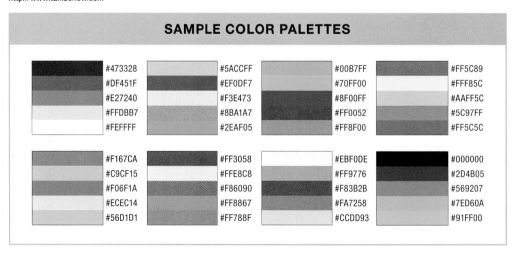

#473328	#5ACCFF	#00B7FF	#FF5C89	
#DF451F	#EF0DF7	#70FF00	#FFF85C	
#E27240	#F3E473	#8F00FF	#AAFF5C	
#FFDBB7	#8BA1A7	#FF0052	#5C97FF	
#FEFFFF	#2EAF05	#FF8F00	#FF5C5C	
#F167CA	#FF3058	#EBF0DE	#000000	
#C9CF15	#FFE8C8	#FF9776	#2D4B05	
#F06F1A	#F86090	#F83B2B	#569207	
#ECEC14	#FF8867	#FA7258	#7ED60A	
#56D1D1	#FF788F	#CCDD93	#91FF00	

06

SITES BY STRUCTURE

A section on site structure may seem out of place in a book meant to inspire, yet the methods used to build the sites in this section are extraordinary. Inspiration is simply the injection of ideas, the altering of our normal paths of thinking. Sometimes we need to be reminded of simple options like being able to scroll horizontally, changing the physical size of site elements or fitting all the content on a single page. And when it comes to old standbys like tabs and drop-down menus, it is easy to see how we might fall into patterns without realizing it. By taking a look at an assortment of structures, we are quickly reminded of our infinite options, despite the apparent limitations.

06

SITES BY STRUCTURE

Horizontal Scrolling
Zoom In Atypical Navigation
Tabs Three Buckets
Modules Tiny
One Page Massive Footers
Atypical Layout
Hybrid

HORIZONTAL SCROLLING

The horizontal scrolling site is a strange little beast. It might be presumed that this design approach is just a desperate attempt to make something unique. But after considering a few good samples, it is clear that horizontal scrolling can be an interesting interface. In fact, it is almost more natural to scroll horizontally than it is to scroll vertically, and in certain situations it fits the content better.

Imagine if the real world worked like the web. Going to an art gallery would require a very strange building that allowed the art to pass by vertically, or an enormous staircase you could climb up and down to view the art. Perhaps this seems like a silly point, but after looking at a few sample sites you will see how natural horizontal scrolling can feel.

The Graphic Therapy site offers a great example of how fluid and pleasant horizontal scrolling can be. Photography is a topic that lends itself very nicely to this style. The images feel like a nice, solid block of photos—very impressive indeed. It would really lose a lot of its presentation power with a vertical layout.

Certainly, some sites use this style as a way to create an interesting new type of layout. Sites like Humor by Jason Love completely break the mold in terms of traditional layout. His site packs most of the content into a single page and starts you in the middle. Finding the content becomes an adventure, and somehow it just works.

Another fine example of photography presented in a horizontal fashion is the Ricky Cox site. Again, the content lends itself to this style of presentation. The vertical nature of most of the photos creates a nice horizontal band. If these had been placed vertically they would have consumed far more space. Additionally, the horizontal placement allows the photos to interact with one other instead of standing individually. Because they are viewed as a whole, they have vivid impact on the viewer.

//GraphicTherapy

Design & Art Direction.

Portfolio   Profile   Connect   Links

Moby Hotel

Global campaign Album.
Client: V2 Records (USA) Mute Records (rest of World)
Photography by Danny Clinch

Verve Remixed

Art Direction + Design
Verve Music Series of Jazz greats remixed by contemporary DJs.
Create Brand System for ongoing collection
Above, 2nd album in series
Photography Rick Swist

http://graphictherapy.com

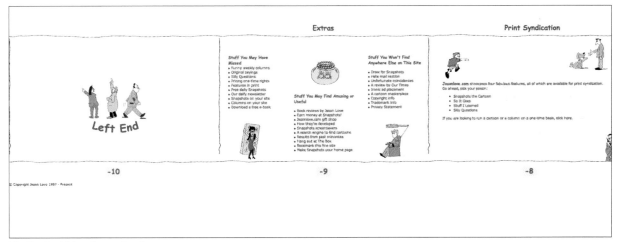

Extras   **Print Syndication**

Stuff You May Have Missed
- Funny weekly columns
- Original sayings
- Silly Questions
- Pricing one-time rights.
- Features in print
- Free daily Snapshots
- Our daily newsletter
- Snapshots on your site
- Columns on your site
- Download a free e-book

Stuff You May Find Amusing or Useful
- Book reviews by Jason Love
- Earn money at Snapshots!
- Jasonlove.com gift shop
- How they're developed
- Snapshots screensavers
- A search engine to find cartoons
- Results from past minivotes
- Hang out at The Box
- Bookmark this fine site
- Make Snapshots your home page

Stuff You Won't Find Anywhere Else on This Site
- Draw for Snapshots
- Hate mail section
- Unfortunate coincidences
- A review by Our Times
- Ironic ad placement
- A cartoon masterpiece
- Copyright info
- Trademark info
- Privacy Statement

Jasonlove.com showcases four fabulous features, all of which are available for print syndication. Go ahead, pick your poison:

- Snapshots the Cartoon
- So It Goes
- Stuff I Learned
- Silly Questions

If you are looking to run a cartoon or a column on a one-time basis, click here.

Left End

−10   −9   −8

© Copyright Jason Love 1997 - Present

http://handmadeinteractive.com/jasonlove

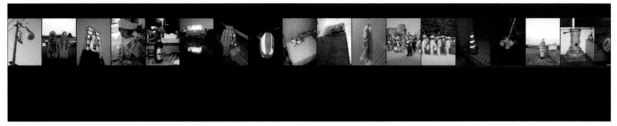

http://www.rickycox.com

http://www.webfellowforhire.com

http://www.miguelperez.es

http://www.bluevertigo.com.ar

http://www.mutanz.com

http://www.peter-hermann.com

http://www.neu-e.de

213

06

SITES BY STRUCTURE

Horizontal Scrolling
Zoom In
Atypical Navigation
Tabs
Three Buckets
Modules
Tiny
One Page
Massive Footers
Atypical Layout
Hybrid

ZOOM IN

On this type of website, you can make selections and zoom in to have the content revealed. You either zoom in on tiny content, or you move the cursor above the content and see parts of it come into your scope of view. This might sound a lot like every single web page out there, but there is a difference. Nearly every site has content that requires scrolling, but the distinction here is that zooming feels more fluid, and it is less reliant on the browser's scroll bars. Just look at a sample or two to get the concept. It is more about creating a flow in the transition between content than it is about jumping from page to page.

The interesting thing about this type of interface is that it encourages visitors to explore. I find myself wanting to see where I can go and what I might find in different sections—sort of like a treasure hunt. A great example of this

is the Jlern Design site: It clearly shows the hierarchy created as you zoom in. In the zoomed-out view, the content is visible but not legible. This connection between the framework and the content is fascinating, and it gives the content a space in which to live.

This is all just a slightly different form of interface than we are used to, and that becomes the real charm of these sites. I think the lesson to learn from these samples is that sometimes a subtle change in the interface can be very beneficial: It gives it a fresh feel without making it obnoxious to navigate. In fact, the navigation in these samples feels downright intuitive, so it could be argued that the layout formula actually makes usage easier. The type of environment these sites create is not revolutionary, but it is simple to understand and adds a great deal of interest.

http://www.jlern.com

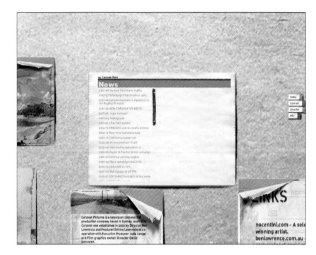

http://www.caravanpictures.com

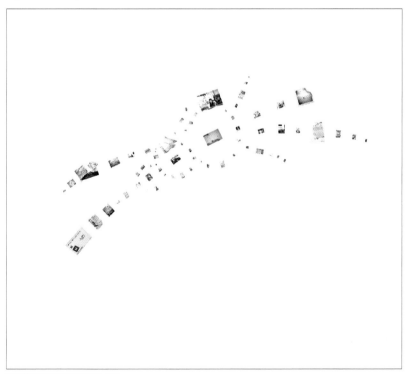

http://www.matthewmahon.com

http://www.javierferrervidal.com

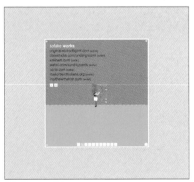

http://www.sofake.com

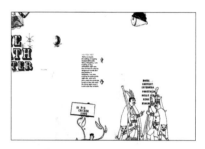

http://www.thebathwater.com

http://www.exponentialdesign.co.uk

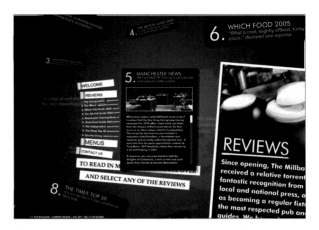

http://www.themillbank.com

http://www.conceptm.nl

http://www.azuna.net

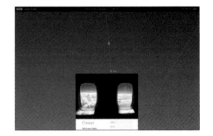

http://www.xrs.pl

http://www.gullyland.com

06
SITES BY STRUCTURE

Horizontal Scrolling
Zoom In
Atypical Navigation
Tabs
Three Buckets
Modules
Tiny
One Page
Massive Footers
Atypical Layout
Hybrid

ATYPICAL NAVIGATION

Developing creative navigation techniques that are easy to use can be a significant challenge. Yielding to the temptation to try creative navigation styles can lead to problems. For this reason, it is important to understand the reasoning behind using such a style. Atypical navigation requires a delicate balance between creativity and practicality. If it gets too crazy, it becomes unusable and incredibly frustrating. That being said, clever navigation can also be so intuitive that it increases usability and becomes a natural part of the site.

Consider the topic of the site. If an unusual navigation style doesn't fit the topic, avoid it at all costs. If, on the other hand, the site is intended to be more of an experience, taking creative steps to merge the navigation into that experience is a great idea. But overall, never lose sight of the fact that people have to figure out how to use the navigation system, and that can be a fun or frustrating experience, depending on what you create.

Consider the target audience. Is this site geared toward kids, adults, seniors … or a mix? Young people tend to figure things out quickly, which makes atypical navigation a more viable option for such audiences. As for seniors, the American population is aging as the baby boomer generation moves into retirement. It is wise to keep this in mind as vision, color and coordination issues become problematic for this audience. In other words, don't rely on confusing navigation styles if you expect seniors to use the site.

Finally, consider the purpose of the site. As previously mentioned, sites meant to create an experience would likely benefit from nontraditional navigation. If, however, the site is intended to provide corporate information to a wide range of people, there is almost no choice but to follow the norm. The standards work well in many cases simply because they do not require users to learn anything new.

Ultimately, look for ways to make this style work for you, especially when it fits the topic in an elegant way. But don't force it. And above all, don't forget that users have to figure out how to work with your creation. Implementing a style that is not intuitive could result in a dead site.

http://www.webdesign20.com

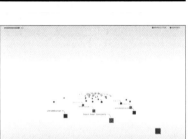

http://www.lmdesign.net

http://www.mandchou.com

10.03.07 New Film Music's Audio Updated
09.14.07 New Concert Music's Audio Updated
09.10.07 Pictures of the Belvedere Festival
06.12.07 Press Release From Berklee's Site
05.28.07 Scoring Garrick

http://www.hmtmx.com

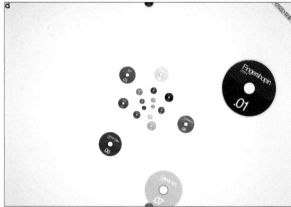

http://a-i.tw

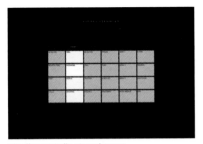
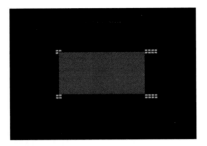

http://www.studio-stemmler.com

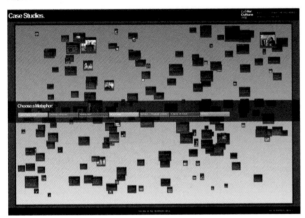
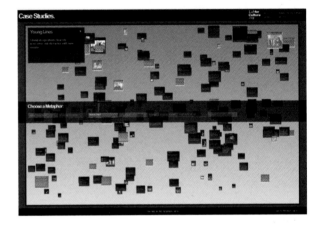

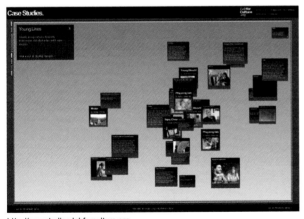
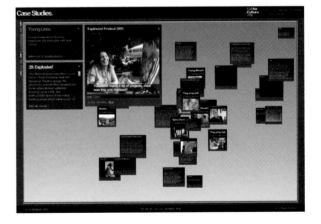

http://casestudies.labforculture.org

06
SITES BY STRUCTURE

Horizontal Scrolling
Zoom In
Atypical Navigation
Tabs
Three Buckets
Modules
Tiny
One Page
Massive Footers
Atypical Layout
Hybrid

TABS

Tabs are basic web design tools, so just about anything and everything has been done to them. I've included examples of some of the most interesting implementations here.

Rotating the traditional tab and putting it vertically on the page is an interesting idea. Prague Design placed its two tabs vertically on the right-hand side of the page with no negative impact. The tabs stand alone in the narrow third column, making them easy to find and use while consuming minimal space.

A more traditional approach to tab design can be found on Newsberry. The tabs on this site have the typical rounded corners. The last tab has been cleverly colored to help it stand out since it contains the key call to action. The shiny effect, the nice little icon and the raised current tab make this site's tabs

a beautiful variation on the traditional tab style.

Tabs are frequently used for literal purposes. An effective example of such literal use is the Esopus Magazine site. The site design revolves around a standard hanging file folder with a bunch of tabs. The site uses tabs to organize content and establish a design theme. Doing so unifies the layout with the concept and purpose of the site.

One last example is the SaraJoy Pond site. Here we find tabs with a stunning design. These tabs have been fashionably designed to fit the style of the site beautifully. All too often, tabs don't bond with a site's design and consequently seem slapped on out of necessity. That is not the case here. These tabs are rich little bits of the design, and they add to the overall appeal of the site.

http://www.praguedesign.cz

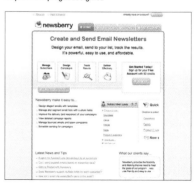

http://newsberry.com

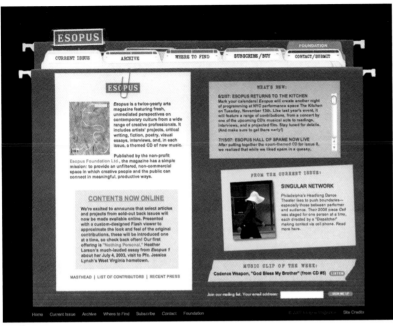

http://www.valentinaolini.com

http://www.babytoothcenter.com

http://rebusiness.com.au

http://esopusmag.com

http://sarajoypond.com

http://www.netresults.com

06

SITES BY STRUCTURE

Horizontal Scrolling
Zoom In
Atypical Navigation
Tabs
Three Buckets
Modules
Tiny
One Page
Massive Footers
Atypical Layout
Hybrid

THREE BUCKETS

It seems there is an endless supply of things that come in threes. The number holds some magic that just plain works. On the web we often find manifestations of threes on homepages: three steps of instructions, three key selling points, three main products, three main options. We love threes. It is the perfect amount of information to consume with ease. Having three options isn't so bad, but having ten options is overwhelming. Sometimes three creeps up to four, and it still works, but it can be very near too much. Three is most certainly the sweet spot.

Often these are action items that contain a button to inspire the user to do something. Consider the fact that these sets of buckets present themselves as a single visual entity. The user then scans through the site. This becomes a major focal point and is the perfect spot to put a call to action. What do you want your users to do? Sign up for an evaluation? Request more information? Register with the site? Whatever it is, this is a perfect spot to encourage users to take the next step.

MochiAds is a perfect demonstration of putting calls to action in the three-bucket arrangement. In this case, the buckets draw the visitor into one of the three key sections of the site. These sections have drastically different goals, so it is important that they help you get to the correct spot quickly. By helping visitors find the information they need, the site minimizes the potential loss of clients and partners.

For a more action-oriented example, take a look at the Business-Paper site. Here, the goal is to direct visitors to information that will convince them to buy the product. Instead of containing tons of product information, the homepage serves as a portal to funnel users to the appropriate sales information for their needs. The third bucket is dedicated to the product tour, which is an excellent sales tool.

http://www.mochiads.com

http://www.ocean70.com

http://business-paper.dk

http://www.nemarkmedia.co.uk

http://www.habitat.org/youthprograms

http://www.orbitshakers.com

http://pdim.net

http://www.koder.cz

http://www.mailandgo.co.uk

06
SITES BY STRUCTURE

Horizontal Scrolling
Zoom In
Atypical Navigation
Tabs
Three Buckets
Modules
Tiny
One Page
Massive Footers
Atypical Layout
Hybrid

MODULES

Designers commonly organize site content by placing it into various containers. Many people find comfort in such order. This compartmentalization connects with viewers and makes it easier to break down content. Humans love order, and nothing brings order like nice little containers. It is possible to contain and separate content without wrapping it in a visual device, but in these samples the designers have done just that by putting each set of content in its own visual module.

Modules can be simple and imageless, or they can have extreme visual style with complex images and expanding boxes. One clever thing to do with these modules is to break the border of its parent container. This is a marvelous idea for two reasons. First, it binds the content together, and second, it brings focus to a certain module or section of the page. To put it simply, modules bring order and hierarchy.

In some cases, modules help break content into usable chunks. Many portal sites make use of this because they contain such a mountain of content. In many ways homepages act as portals to all the content a site contains. One such example is EntertainmentAfrica. This homepage has a massive amount of links. The clear organization created by the modules helps visitors cut through the clutter to find the content they are looking for.

Another site that creates a highly scannable design via modules is the Havoc Studios site. By placing the content into clear modules with prominent labels, users can scan for and find the content they are looking for. In this case, the most recent content is appropriately highlighted and easy to find. This helps returning visitors find the fresh content without being distracted by old news.

http://www.entertainmentafrica.com

http://www.havocstudios.co.uk

http://www.listentomanchester.co.uk

http://www.churchmedia.cc

http://www.gagles.com.br

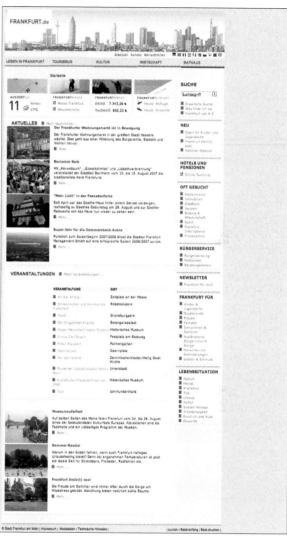

http://www.frankfurt.de

http://www.blacktomato.co.uk

06
SITES BY STRUCTURE

Horizontal Scrolling
Zoom In
Atypical Navigation
Tabs
Three Buckets
Modules
Tiny
One Page
Massive Footers
Atypical Layout
Hybrid

TINY

Sometimes a website is necessary but doesn't require much content. In this case, a tiny site might be in order. Simple contact or resume sites don't have heaps of information to post. Use that lack of content to your advantage and pack all the information into a consumable micro-container. This approach is all about turning a problem into the solution!

Pocket Web Site is a prime example of how this style can be a great success. The creator had such a small amount of information to communicate that it could all be contained in a matchbook, so that is exactly how the site is styled. It can be exasperating to come up with lots of copy for a small site. Pocket Web Site found a clever solution to this problem by playing off the idea of being small.

Another tasty example of this style is SushiBeads. This site is small in size, but not in style. Despite its lack of bloated content, the creators embellished this design with a gorgeous wrapper that gives it a life far beyond its meager size. In this case, it is fun that the small site plays into the idea of tiny beads. Overall, it is a tremendous success.

One example that seems to contain a more typical set of content is Nicolas Huon's personal site. It contains all the expected information and more than fills itself out, yet it has remained very tiny. This really goes to show how much unnecessary fluff ends up on many sites. This style forced the creator to cut to the chase and allow only the meaty content onto the site.

http://www.nicolashuon.info

http://www.sushibeads.com

http://www.pocketwebsite.net

http://www.espaciozero.com

http://www.creativeireland.com

http://workbench-music.com

http://www.tolgaerbay.com

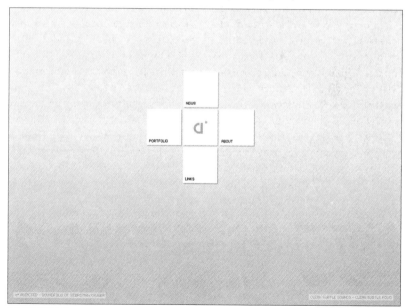

http://audicted.de

06
SITES BY STRUCTURE

Horizontal Scrolling *Zoom In* *Atypical Navigation* *Tabs* *Three Buckets* *Modules* *Tiny* **One Page** *Massive Footers* *Atypical Layout* *Hybrid*

ONE PAGE

The one-page website is the epitome of efficiency. It lumps all of the content into a single page. Clearly this will not work in every case, but for many situations it is a great idea. However, it is an idea that usually isn't considered. One situation that lends itself perfectly to the single page is the portfolio site.

A portfolio site's goal is to grab the attention of someone who is potentially going to pay the site's owner to do work. It seems there are two key elements to make this happen. First, the portfolio and content must be presented in the best possible environment. This is especially important for those who are in the business of making things look good. Creative types clearly have to do their best to make their portfolios stand out visually while showing their work in the best possible light. It is critical that their site stand apart from the herd. Second, the site should enable visitors to see the work as easily as possible. In this way the one-page portfolio really starts to make sense. A nice, long flow of beautiful images is very powerful. By putting everything in one page it is harder for potential employers to overlook the samples that would impress them.

In nonportfolio situations, the single-page site can still make sense: It is a great way to avoid complicating things that don't need to be. You shouldn't force this style onto a site, but in many cases there simply isn't enough content to justify more than one page. This can be a tough sell to a client, considering the fact that most people presume sites should have many pages to be taken seriously, even if there isn't sufficient content to fill them.

One particularly fun example of the one-page style site is Didoo. Here, the designer has broken the content into three chunks. This could have easily been a three-page site, but there isn't enough content in each section to justify three separate pages. By putting everything into one page, the designer creates a streamlined process for consuming the site. And viewers don't feel overwhelmed with too much content because it is organized in nice little groupings.

http://www.didoo.net

http://www.nickdeakin.com

http://anatolip.com

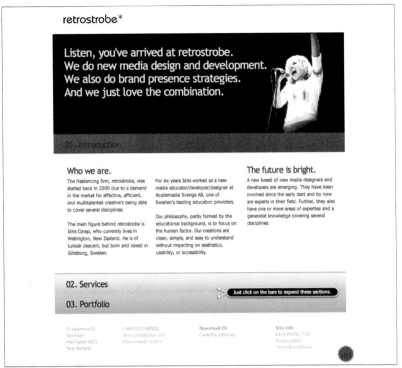

http://www.retrostrobe.com

http://www.booreiland.nl

http://lukestevensdesign.com

http://www.sromek.cz

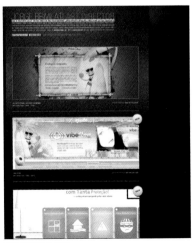

http://brivilati.com

http://www.philippseifried.com

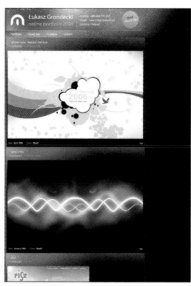

http://www.grondecki.pl/portfolio.html

http://www.laksman.com.ar

http://www.allankirsten.com

http://www.ryanjclose.com

06

SITES BY STRUCTURE

Horizontal Scrolling Zoom In Atypical Navigation Tabs Three Buckets Modules Tiny One Page **Massive Footers** Atypical Layout Hybrid

MASSIVE FOOTERS

The footer is an often-overlooked element. In most cases, it is the place on the page where a few random legal links are dumped and forgotten. In fact, the footers of most sites serve no purpose beyond framing the page. This is tragic because the footer can be put to good use. As users read content and reach the bottom of a page they will likely look for the next step. Should they buy the product? Perhaps read another article? I am sure that the site's goal is not to get users to read copyright information, so why end every single page on a site this way?

Some sites have already considered this. Take a look at the Doug Dosberg

site, for example. This site has a huge footer stuffed with good information. In fact, the footer is so big it is nearly a full screen of information on small monitors. Sure, the footer contains the usual copyright mumbo jumbo, but it also contains a list of information that may interest users after they finish reading the current article. In this way, it serves as a pointer to next steps.

The moral of the story is to think of a website as a series of pages, not just as individual, single-page experiences. So much thought goes into the layout of a page and how the user will interact with it that not enough energy is put into next steps at the end of the page.

http://www.dougdosberg.com

http://www.touristr.com

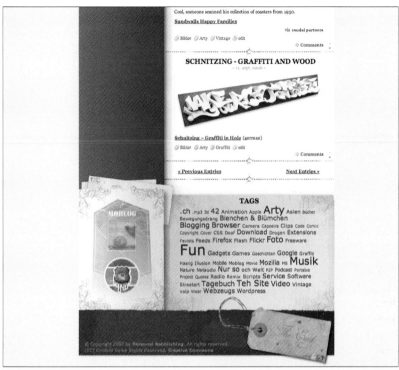

http://sis.slowli.com

http://www.larissameek.com

http://www.asfusion.com

http://businesslogs.com

http://www.elliotswan.com

http://www.vagrantradio.com

Horizontal Scrolling
Zoom In
Atypical Navigation
Tabs
Three Buckets
Modules
Tiny
One Page
Massive Footers
Atypical Layout
Hybrid

ATYPICAL LAYOUT

In all segments of the creative industry, designers are always on the lookout for fresh ideas and new ways of doing old things. It is refreshing to learn fun ways to mix things up and break through the visual clutter, if only to avoid the inevitable boredom that comes from doing the same layouts over and over again. This set of sites contains samples that have taken risks. Some of these layouts are more practical than others, and it is possible that a client would not approve of some of them either. It doesn't hurt to get those gears churning, though, as radical ideas often lead to subtle changes that cause a shift in design patterns.

Often, simple shifts in the placement of things can result in completely fresh designs that are still easy to use. A great example of this is the moodboard site. This layout is by no means radically unique, but it does show a distinct shift from standard formats. For example, the search box is typically located in the top right corner. On moodboard, it is placed near the top left. In this case, it not only makes the site visually distinct, but it also increases functionality. Its atypical location actually draws more attention to it, which makes searching for photos on the site even easier. This is perfect, since this is the whole point of the site.

Another fantastic example of atypical layout is the VTKS Design site. The purpose of this site is to showcase the artist's work. So instead of a standard navigation scheme, the artist basically made the first image an attention-grabbing hook. Why present such beautiful and eye-catching artwork in a standard, grid-based layout? Sure, as you dig into the site, you get more structure. All the same, the site showcases the artist's work in a clever, nontraditional format. Interestingly, this plays into the artist's rebellious, underground style. The real beauty of the site is that despite its completely nonstandard layout, navigation is a breeze.

http://www.vtks.com.br

http://www.zeppenfeld.com

http://www.moodboard.com

http://www.bigsquaredot.com

http://www.trout.com.au

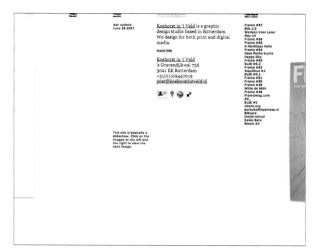

http://www.koehorstintveld.nl

http://www.michaelfakesch.com

http://tinyteam.com

06
SITES BY STRUCTURE

Horizontal Scrolling
Zoom In
Atypical Navigation
Tabs
Three Buckets
Modules
Tiny
One Page
Massive Footers
Atypical Layout
Hybrid

HYBRID

Mixing Flash and standard HTML elements is commonly referred to as a hybrid style of site development. This isn't so much a design element as it is a technique for building. However, this style of building actually plays into design completely, as it is typically done to enhance the design of a site.

Flash began with a bang, and many sites went pure Flash. Since then, Flash has shifted greatly and is now mainly used on hybrid sites. This makes perfect sense when you consider the various benefits of each medium. By combining the core benefits of the two technologies—the dynamics of Flash with the practicality of HTML—you can avoid many of the pitfalls of using only one or the other. With content primarily in HTML, there is no need to worry about search engines indexing a site. And Flash offers much more enticing visual elements and presentation style abilities.

The Digitalmash site offers a perfect example of Flash that is so tightly integrated that it is impossible to tell where it starts. Ultra-tight integration such as this is amazing. The concept is simple, though. Just take an element of the design and animate it in some way using Flash. This creates a memorable dynamic on the page. In the case of the Digitalmash site, the page is literally brought to life. An otherwise nice design then becomes something to be remembered and perhaps even talked about. Another more common approach is to have a nice bit of Flash that fits the site but isn't incorporated so seamlessly. Ben Saunders expertly demonstrates this technique. The Flash movie on the homepage completely fits the design of the site even though it is clear that it is an isolated portion of the page. This is not a bad thing; it is just a far more common approach. The Flash movie brings a level of interest to the homepage that it would not have if it were entirely static.

The richness and visual interest of such tools certainly bring these sites to life in a way that HTML alone never could. The beauty of this is that Flash has been used to enhance a traditional website that would never have been done completely in Flash. In this way the benefits of both Flash and HTML are enjoyed, and an overall better site is the result.

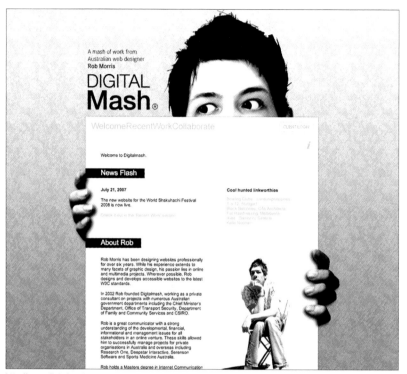

http://www.digitalmash.com

http://www.bensaunders.com

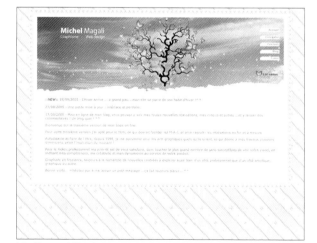

http://dogoworld.free.fr

http://www.iris-interactive.fr

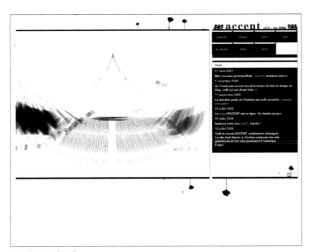

http://accent.free.fr

http://www.its.com.uy

http://www.brandneusense.com

http://www.novalux.com

http://anniesgourmetkitchen.net

INDEX/PERMISSIONS

p. 042 **http://www.aiderss.com** AideRSS, Inc. © 2007
p. 042 **http://www.formsite.com** Vroman Systems, Inc. © 2007
p. 042 **http://heywatch.com** Hey!Watch © 2007
p. 044 **http://www.campaignmonitor.com** Freshview © 2007
p. 044 **http://www.bigcartel.com** Matt Wigham © 2007
p. 044 **http://www.tickspot.com** Molehill © 2007
p. 045 **http://www.simplyinvoices.com** roobasoft, LLC © 2007
p. 045 **http://www.slimtimer.com** Richard White © 2007
p. 045 **http://www.feelbreeze.com** ElementFusion © 2007
p. 045 **http://www.mochibot.com** Mochi Media, Inc. © 2007
p. 045 **http://www.lessaccounting.com** Less Everything, inc © 2007
p. 045 **http://www.relenta.com** © Relenta 2007
p. 046 **http://crazyegg.com** Crazy Egg, Inc. © 2007
p. 046 **http://www.cogmap.com** CogMap © 2007
p. 046 **http://squirl.info** Squirl LLC © 2007
p. 046 **http://pbwiki.com** © 2007 PBwiki
p. 046 **http://www.santexq.com** AR Santex, LLC © 2007
p. 049 **http://www.targetscope.com** TargetScope © 2007
p. 049 **http://www.cakephp.org** CakePHP Software Foundation © 2007
p. 049 **http://rockbeatspaper.net** Rockbeatspaper © 2007
p. 049 **http://www.targetscopehosting.com** TargetScope Hosting, Inc. © 2007
p. 050 **http://www.wddg.com** WDDG, Inc. © 2006
p. 050 **http://www.detektiv-nali.de** All rights reserved Detektiv Nali © 2007
p. 050 **http://www.bombippy.com** Jay Kerr © 2007
p. 050 **http://www.mondomochales.com** Content: Enrique Mochales © 2007. Design: www.vudumedia.com © 2007
p. 050 **http://www.fontdiner.com** © 2007 Font Diner, Inc
p. 050 **http://www.maniacmonkeymedia.com** Maniac Monkey Media © 2007
p. 051 **http://www.puchlerz.com** © 2004-2007 Matt Puchlerz. All rights reserved.
p. 051 **http://dollardreadful.com** W. Staehle & T.D. Rio © 2007
p. 052 **http://www.tbgd.co.uk** tbgd © 2007
p. 052 **http://www.endcommunications.com** End Communications, LLC © 2007
p. 053 **http://www.studiorobot.com.au** Studio Robot © 2007
p. 053 **http://microformatique.com** John Allsopp © 2007
p. 053 **http://minifolio.binaryvein.com** Binary Vein Digital Media © 2007
p. 053 **http://www.captured.nu** Systm Global Aesthetic Conditioning © 2007
p. 054 **http://www.filosof.biz** Jan Řezáč © 2007
p. 054 **http://androo.com** Andrew Lin © 2007
p. 054 **http://www.openedhand.com** OpenedHand Ltd © 2007
p. 054 **http://www.terracestudios.co.uk** Ewan Robertson © 2007
p. 055 **http://www.spacemakerwardrobes.com.au** Spacemaker Wardrobes Pty Ltd © 2007
p. 055 **http://pixelpanic.be** Tijs Vrolix © 2007
p. 056 **http://lab.arc90.com** Arc90, Inc. © 2007
p. 056 **http://www.coreaudiovisual.com** John Dames / coreaudiovisual © 2007
p. 056 **http://www.clandrei.de** clandrei GmbH © 2006
p. 056 **http://www.period-three.com** Period Three, LLC © 2007
p. 056 **http://www.whalesalad.com** © 2007 Michael Whalen
p. 056 **http://www.mediact.nl** © 2007 mediaCT webinterieur
p. 056 **http://www.protolize.org** Protolize.org © 2007
p. 056 **http://simplebits.com** SimpleBits, LLC © 2007
p. 057 **http://new-bamboo.co.uk** New Bamboo Web Development Ltd © 2007
p. 057 **http://www.achtentachtig** Achtentachtig © 2007

p. 057 **http://www.joshclarkportfolio.com** Josh Clark © 2007
p. 059 **http://www.urban-international.com** Timm Kekeritz © 2005
p. 059 **http://wwwthwave.co.uk** 9thwave New Media © 2007
p. 059 **http://www.sourhaze.comv7** Elliot Jay Stocks © 2007
p. 059 **http://www.designsbypatima.com** Patima Tantiprasut © 2007
p. 060 **http://www.beyondjazz.net** Lennart Schoors & Jurriaan Persyn © 2007
p. 060 **http://www.imotion-media.nleng** iMotion Media © 2007
p. 060 **http://www.satsu.co.uk** Satsu Ltd © 2007
p. 060 **http://www.akanai.com** Akanai mediadesign © 2007
p. 060 **http://www.jasonsantamaria.com** Jason Santa Maria © 2004
p. 060 **http://www.kutztown.edu/acad/commdes** Kutztown University of Pennsylvania © 2005
p. 060 **http://www.bitflydesign.com** Mark Tuleweit © 2007
p. 061 **http://strzibny.name/strzibny** Josef Strzibny © 2007
p. 061 **http://www.triplux.com** Michael Green © 2007
p. 063 **http://www.colinmckinney.co.uk** Colin McKinney © 2007
p. 063 **http://www.peepshow.org.uk** Peepshow Collective Ltd © 2007
p. 063 **http://schroeder-wendt.com** www.schroeder-wendt.com © 2007
p. 063 **http://www.softgray.com** ©2007 Soft Gray
p. 063 **http://www.thomasmarban.com** Thomas Marban © 2007
p. 063 **http://www.noodlebox.be** noodlebox © 2007
p. 063 **http://www.cubedesigners.com** Cubedesigners © 2007
p. 063 **http://www.gonzales.be** Sacha Krinstinsky © 2007
p. 065 **http://www.kinoz.com** Andrea Banchini - Kino © 2007
p. 065 **http://www.kinetic.com.sg** kinetic © 2007
p. 065 **http://www.cambrianhouse.com** Cambrian House Inc. © 2006
p. 065 **http://www.thebutchershop.com.au** The Butcher Shop and Studio Robot © 2007
p. 066 **http://tim.samoff.com** Creative Commons Attribution-NoDerivs 3.0
p. 066 **http://www.artinhk.com** Sino Group© 2007
p. 066 **http://www.midwestisbest.com** Michael Perry © 2007
p. 066 **http://smallfriescookbook.com** Teri Studios © 2007
p. 066 **http://www.mathildeaubier.free.fr** Mathilde Aubier © 2007
p. 066 **http://www.melkadel.com** Mel Kadel © 2007
p. 067 **http://www.rmusic.co.uk** retna UK © 2007
p. 068 **http://www.timeforcake.com** timeforcake creative media, inc. © 2007
p. 068 **http://www.fracture.co.nz** Fracture Media Syndicate Ltd. © 2007
p. 068 **http://44suburbia.org** Melissa Miller © 2007
p. 068 **http://www.yozzan.com** Copyright www.yozzan.com © 2007
p. 068 **http://d3zin3.net** d3zn3.net© 2007
p. 069 **http://stolendesign.net** Jesse Steinfort © 2007
p. 069 **http://www.atelierdetour.ch** Atelier Détour © 2007
p. 069 **http://www.tylergaw.com** Tyler Gaw © 2007
p. 071 **http://www.intuitivedesigns.net** Intuitive Designs © 2007
p. 071 **http://web.burza.hr/** web.burza © 2007
p. 071 **http://www.octonauts.com** Meomi Design © 2007
p. 071 **http://www.brentayers.com** Brent Ayers © 2007
p. 072 **http://www.keithandlottie.com** Keith + Lottie and Studio Robot © 2007
p. 072 **http://multimedia.valenciacc.edu** Graphics Technology | Valencia Community College © 2007
p. 072 **http://www.areeba.com.au** Areeba Solutions Pty Ltd © 2007
p. 072 **http://www.smallandround.com** Jeremiah Ketner © 2007

p. 072 **http://www.leuyenpham.com** LeUyen Pham © 2007
p. 072 **http://www.aquaboogie.net** AquaBoogie Design Studio © 2007
p. 072 **http://deborahcavenaugh.com** Deborah Cavenaugh Studio © 2007
p. 072 **http://www.philinehartert.com** Philine Hartert © 2007
p. 074 **http://www.decomart.co.uk** Grzegorz Szostak © 2007
p. 074 **http://wwwadvanced.com** 2Advanced Studios, LLC. © 2007
p. 074 **http://www.analogue.ca** Analogue © 2007
p. 074 **http://www.evoland.es** www.evoland.es © 2007
p. 074 **http://www.designandimage.com** Design and Image Communications © 2007
p. 075 **http://pedrosdiveclub.com** Peter Lawrence © 2007
p. 075 **http://www.superieur-graphique.com** sven stueber 4 superieur-graphique.com © 2007
p. 075 **http://www.herbatonica.com** domenico catapano © 2007
p. 075 **http://www.swivelheaddesign.com** © 2007 Swivelhead Design Works, LLC
p. 075 **http://www.secondstory.com** © 2007 Second Story Inc.
p. 077 **http://www.getfinch.com** Francisco Inchauste © 2007
p. 077 **http://www.jeffreydocherty.com** Jeffrey Docherty © 2007
p. 077 **http://www.plainsimple.dk** Jonas Priesum © 2007
p. 077 **http://www.citrus7.com.br** Citrus7 © 2007
p. 077 **http://www.organicgrid.com** Copyright © 2007. Organic Grid. All rights reserved.
p. 077 **http://www.bureausla.nl** Het Gelaat © 2007
p. 077 **http://www.martinkonrad.com.au** Martin Konrad © 2007
p. 077 **http://blogsolid.com** Blogsolid © Imar Krige 2007
p. 077 **http://www.darrenalawi.com** © 2007 darrenalawi™
p. 079 **http://www.vanhoning.nl** van honing © 2007
p. 079 **http://designgraphy.com** DESIGNGRAPHY.COM © 2007
p. 079 **http://www.danielsantiago.com** Daniel Santiago © 2007
p. 079 **http://www.mattmo.com** Mattmo concept i design © 2007
p. 079 **http://www.jp33.com** jp33 - Jeremy Prasatik © 2007
p. 080 **http://www.wrecked.nu** Gabriel Rubin © 2007
p. 080 **http://adellecharles.com** Adelle Charles © 2007
p. 080 **http://www.sergiojuncos.com** Sergio Juncos © 2007
p. 080 **http://www.pixelshop.org** Brian Faust © 2007
p. 080 **http://chromogenic.net** Justin Ouellette © 2007
p. 080 **http://www.collision-theory.com** collision theory © 2007
p. 080 **http://www.dnna.net** Daniel Skrobak © 2007
p. 083 **http://www000k.com** © 2006 3000k, Inc.
p. 083 **http://www.thisisgrow.com** © 2007 Grow Interactive
p. 083 **http://wwwgrados.comblog** 9grados © 2007
p. 083 **http://mezzanineapp.comblog** mezzanine © 2007
p. 083 **http://www.zachklein.com** Zach Klein © 2007
p. 083 **http://www.bensky.co.uk** BenSky.co.uk © 2007
p. 083 **http://www.hrasti.com** Martin Papazov & Miglena Papazova © 2007
p. 083 **http://www.holdsworthdesign.com** Brian Holdsworth © 2007
p. 084 **http://www.ysprod.com** Yvonne Suberamaniam YS Productions © 2007
p. 084 **http://www.jochemvanwetten.nl** Jochem van Wetten © 2007
p. 084 **http://www.godfarm.org** Copyright © 2005-2007 GodFarm.org. All rights reserved
p. 085 **http://www.pearhosting.com** Pear Hosting © 2007
p. 085 **http://www.tastyapps.com** TastyApps © 2007
p. 086 **http://www.emanuelblagonic.com** Emanuel Blagonic © 2006 - 2007
p. 086 **http://www.kristinejanssen.com** Kristine Jubeck © 2007
p. 086 **http://www.jasonlimon.com** © 2007, Jason Limon
p. 086 **http://www.postmodernsong.org** Denise Moriya © 2007
p. 087 **http://shut.elmota.com** Shut Theory © 2007

p. 087 **http://paperworks.com** Elizabeth Perkowski © 2007
p. 088 **http://www.switchinteractive.com** Switch Interactive © 2007
p. 088 **http://www.dobriduhovi.com** plastikfantastik © 2007
p. 088 **http://www.alterform.com** Nate Cavanaugh © 2007
p. 088 **http://www.pilarpunzano.com** Mario Bastian © 2007
p. 088 **http://www.smoothpiece.net** Brett Nyquist © 2007
p. 088 **http://www.ajmiles.net** ajmiles.net © 2007
p. 089 **http://www.boatwerksrestaurant.com** Drew Yeaton, Sentinel Design Group © 2007
p. 089 **http://www.johnphillipslive.com** John Philips © 2007
p. 089 **http://www.plankdesign.comen** © Plank 2007
p. 091 **http://www.pupstyle.com** PupStyle.com © 2004-2007
p. 091 **http://www.unstructure.com** Keegan Rooney © 2007
p. 091 **http://www.freshbrew.com** FreshBrew, Inc. © 2007
p. 091 **http://www.backfrog.com** Sung Choi © 2007
p. 091 **http://www.designtrance.com** designtrance © 2007
p. 091 **http://www.craig-russell.co.uk** Craig Russell © 2007
p. 091 **http://www.ustvarjalko.si** plastikfantastik © 2007
p. 092 **http://www.joshuakristal.com** Joshua Kristal © 2007
p. 092 **http://www.logicalbinary.com** logicalbinary © 2007
p. 094 **http://www.iso50.com** Scott Hansen / ISO50 © 2007
p. 094 **http://electricpulp.com** © 2007 Electric Pulp. All rights reserved. Electric Pulp is a registered trademark.
p. 094 **http://www.draftmedia.de** Thomas Schröpfer - draft. media © 2007
p. 094 **http://kanalydesign.com** Kanaly Design © 2007
p. 094 **http://skullsandcandy.com** Skulls and Candy © 2007
p. 094 **http://granthelton.com** Grant Helton © 2007
p. 094 **http://www.mondayrunner.com** Tim van den Bosch © 2007
p. 094 **http://www.capitolmedia.com** Capitol Media, Inc © 2007
p. 095 **http://www.est1977.com** andy alexander © 2007
p. 095 **http://www.delicious-monster.com** Delicious Monster Software, LLC © 2007
p. 097 **http://wp-design.org** WP-Design © 2007
p. 097 **http://www.mac3dsoftware.com** David Ellis © 2007
p. 097 **http://www.nuage-et-nougatine.com** nuage & nougatine - PiMou © 2007
p. 097 **http://www.bayoukidsdirectory.com** Bayou Region Family & Kids © 2007
p. 097 **http://www.friendsofheathergrossman.com** Angela Rohner © 2007
p. 098 **http://meehantherapy.com** meehantherapy © 2007
p. 098 **http://www.redchess.com** Ed Symington © 2007
p. 099 **http://fendyzaidan.blogspot.com** beckzaidan © 2007
p. 099 **http://www.producemedia.com** producemedia © 2007
p. 100 **http://www.organiclevel.com** Kenny Lidström © 2007
p. 100 **http://www.drewwarkentin.com** Drew Warkentin © 2007
p. 100 **http://www.creativebox.ro** CreativeBox © 2007
p. 100 **http://www.pitstopradio.be** Mei Van Walleghem © 2007
p. 100 **http://www.artworksgroup.net** Artworksgroup © 2007
p. 100 **http://www.myonlyworkingeye.co.uk** © 2007 Oezcan and Jones
p. 100 **http://www.janbrasna.com** © Jan Brašna
p. 100 **http://www.latelier-web.fr** latelier-web.fr© 2007
p. 101 **http://www.peminoz.com** Copyright © 2004-2007 Stuart Hall. All Rights Reserved.
p. 101 **http://www.thevillage.nl** twisted.nl © 2007
p. 101 **http://www.km4042.de** KM4042 © 2004
p. 103 **http://moultonstudio.com** David R. Moulton © 2007
p. 103 **http://www.critbuns.com** Joe Gebbia © 2007
p. 103 **http://www.seydesign.com** seyDoggy © 2007-2008
p. 103 **http://sunsad.de** Bastian Posniak © 2007
p. 103 **http://www.erikmazzone.com** Erik Mazzone © 2007
p. 103 **http://www.dpivision.com** dpivision.com Ltd © 2007

p. 103 **http://www.teamviget.com** Viget Labs © 2007
p. 103 **http://www.dailygrind.it** Sergio Martino © 2007
p. 104 **http://www.itisblank.com** Griskevicius Jurgis © 2007
p. 104 **http://www.tipoos.com** TIPOOS © 2007
p. 104 **http://www.untiedshoes.com** untiedshoes © 2007
p. 106 **http://www.lime.ee** Lime Creative © 2003-2007
p. 106 **http://www.graynode.com** GrayNode © 2000-2007
p. 106 **http://www.gapersblock.com** Gapers Block Media LLC © 2007
p. 106 **http://nationalgazette.org** National Gazette © 2007
p. 106 **http://www.feaverish.com** Aaron Feaver © 2007
p. 106 **http://www.cirut.pl** CIRUTdesign © 2007
p. 106 **http://www.rosefu.net** © 2007 Rose Fu
p. 107 **http://www.book-of-numbers.com** BubblyNumbers © 2006
p. 107 **http://www.e-knjige.net** Trinet racunalne usluge © 2007
p. 107 **http://savremenaginekologija.com** Milica Sekulic © 2007 http://milicasekulic.com
p. 109 **http://idesyns.com** © 2007 Craig Skoney - idesyns.com
p. 109 **http://www.romaingruner.com** Romain Gruner © 2007
p. 109 **http://www.thelume.com** lumus design © 2007
p. 109 **http://www.moodbuilder.com** Key NG © 2007
p. 109 **http://www.bullseyecreative.net** Bullseye Creative © 2006
p. 109 **http://crew.netsuperstar.com** Sascha André Lanninger © 2007
p. 110 **http://www.arienneboelens.nl** Ariënne Boelens© 2007
p. 110 **http://astrostudios.com** ASTRO Studios, Inc. © 2007
p. 110 **http://piotrowskimichal.com** piotrowskimichal © 2007
p. 110 **http://onemillionpod.com** Copyright © 2007 Kashmir Creative
p. 111 **http://www.silasklein.com** silasklein.com © 2007
p. 111 **http://www.foxie.ru** Marina A. Karlova © 2005
p. 111 **http://www.ioworks.org** Ioworks © 2007
p. 111 **http://www.notsosimpleton.com** TheFragileCircus/ Myron Campbell © 2007
p. 111 **http://www.iconinc.com.au** Icon.Inc © 2007
p. 113 **http://www.visitcascadia.com** ©Freightliner LLC 2007: A Pop Art, Inc. Production 2007
p. 113 **http://www.indigo6.comsite2006** Indigo 6, LLC. © 2007
p. 113 **http://www.dizzain.com** Dizzain Inc. © 2007
p. 113 **http://www.funneldesigngroup.com** Funnel Design Group © 2007
p. 113 **http://www.inyourelement.org** copyright © 2007 Champion Forest Baptist Church
p. 114 **http://www.webtreasure.eu** webtreasure.eu © 2007
p. 114 **http://egypt.ebeling.ee/panoramas** Andrei Bodrov © 2007
p. 114 **http://saizenmedia.com** SAIZEN MEDIA STUDIOS | All Rights Reserved © 2007
p. 114 **http://www.joblankenburg.comenglish** Jo Blankenburg © 2007
p. 117 **http://www.digitaldevotion.de** © 2007 Klaus Lehmann
p. 117 **http://www.macminds.net** momono.nl & macminds. net © 2007
p. 117 **http://www.bigfilebox.com** BigBox Software © 2007
p. 117 **http://blog.articlestudio.ca** Luce Beaulieu © 2007
p. 117 **http://www.foan82.com** Foan © 2007
p. 117 **http://www.codepink4peace.org** Farida Sheralam © 2007
p. 118 **http://www.daleharris.com** © Dale Harris 2007
p. 118 **http://www.sofiaregalo.com** sofiaregalo © 2006
p. 118 **http://www.bowwowlondon.com** Bow Wow International Ltd © 2007. All Rights Reserved.
p. 118 **http://www.themissinglink.nl** Edwart Visser, The Missing Link © 2007
p. 120 **http://www.wurkit.com** Daniel Ritzenthaler © 2007
p. 120 **http://www.ilas.com** ilas © 2007
p. 120 **http://www.stephano.se** Stephano © 2007

p. 120 **http://www.sonze.com** Sonze Design Studio © 2007
p. 120 **http://www.dan03.net** Dan 0 © 2007
p. 120 **http://www.gearboxmedia.com** Gearbox Media Ltd © 2007
p. 121 **http://www.youthagainstsudoku.com** Eino Korkala © 2007
p. 121 **http://www.heuserkampf.com** © 2007 Kai Heuser
p. 121 **http://www.hellomuller.com** Tom Muller © 2007
p. 123 **http://www.designerinaction.de** Marco Rullkoetter, Dirk Rullkoetter © 2007
p. 123 **http://www.ignite-imd.com** William D. Creech, Jr. © 2007
p. 123 **http://www.beansbox.com** BeansBox © 2007
p. 123 **http://generationchurch.org** The City Church © 2007
p. 124 **http://www.enhancedlabs.com** Enhanced Labs © 2007
p. 124 **http://spousenotes.com** Ryan Keberly © 2007
p. 124 **http://www.inmo-site.net** Jorge Rausell Díaz-Pavón © 2007
p. 124 **http://www.denyingphoenix.com** Brian Faust © 2007
p. 124 **http://www.popstalin.com** Pop Stalin Design © 2007
p. 125 **http://www.no-spec.com** no-spec.com © 2007
p. 125 **http://www.hellobard.com** HelloBard © 2007
p. 126 **http://www.hive.com.au** copyright 2007 HIVE Creative
p. 126 **http://www.twistsystems.co.uk** Twist Systems Limited © 2007
p. 126 **http://yellowlane.com** Josh Williams © 2007
p. 126 **http://ttcrew.free.fr** TTcrew © 2004-2007
p. 128 **http://www.netprofitservices.com** NetProfitServices. com © 2007
p. 128 **http://www.haveamint.com** Copyright © 2004-2007 Shaun Inman
p. 128 **http://www.jam-factory.com** Gavin Strange © 2007
p. 128 **http://www.alexpaulo.com** alexpaulo.com © 2007
p. 129 **http://www.kokodigital.co.uk** Koko Digital Ltd © 2007
p. 129 **http://www.thruthewoods.com** James Gunardson © 2007
p. 129 **http://www.yourcom.nl** Victor Hopman © 2007
p. 129 **http://www.xhtmlit.com** InterDevil.com © 2007 All Rights Reserved.
p. 130 **http://www.vrebosch.be** Robarov © 2007
p. 130 **http://blogactionday.org** Eden Creative Communities © 2007
p. 132 **http://www.centrigy.com** Copyright © 2006-2007 Centrigy Networks
p. 132 **http://marylandmedia.com** Martin Ringlein © 2007
p. 132 **http://www.inspirebrand.com** Inspire © 2007
p. 132 **http://www.bartelme.at** Wolfgang Bartelme © 2007
p. 132 **http://www.madmilk.com** Copyright © 2007 Madmilk. All rights reserved.
p. 133 **http://www.mav.com.pl** M.Bazentkiewicz Maver!cK © 2007
p. 133 **http://www.microico.com** KoreKogic © 2007
p. 133 **http://michalsobel.pomeranc.cz** Michal Sobel © 2007
p. 133 **http://www.myquire.com** Quire Inc. © 2007
p. 133 **http://www.usemime.com** Trust5 © 2007
p. 134 **http://www.eutelnet.biz** EUtelNet © 2007
p. 134 **http://emanuelfelipe.net** Emanuel Felipe © 2007
p. 136 **http://marios.tziortzis.comphotoblog** Marios Tziortzis © 2007
p. 136 **http://www.tndmedia.nl** TND media © 2007
p. 136 **http://www.dream-design.net** Bel Koo © 2007
p. 136 **http://www.purple2pink.com** purple2pink © 2007
p. 137 **http://www.tapsonic.com** tapsonic © 2007
p. 137 **http://www.fireflyfoundation.org** All content is © Firefly™ 2006.
p. 137 **http://www.espiratecnologias.com** Espira Tecnologías Web © 2007
p. 137 **http://www.avantgrape.com** avantGRAPE © 2008
p. 139 **http://www.quo.com.au** Adam Morris, Saul Jarvie, Simon Litchfield © 2007

p. 139 **http://www.envirocorplabs.com** Allen Hopper © 2007
p. 139 **http://www.alphanumeric.cz** © 2000-2007 Alphanumeric
p. 139 **http://www.ploink-brothers.com** ZOZ © 2007
p. 140 **http://www8d.se** Mario Eklund © 2007
p. 140 **http://www.okapistudio.com** OkapiStudio © 2007
p. 140 **http://www.cloigheann.com** Mission Data © 2007
p. 140 **http://www.krabi.ee** Tõnu Runnel © 2006
p. 141 **http://www.terrabaltica.lv/en** Terra Baltica Travel © 2007
p. 141 **http://www.blastadvancedmedia.com** Blast Advanced Media © 2007
p. 141 **http://www.tyrcha.com** Scott Tyrcha, Jr. © 2007
p. 143 **http://mattbrett.com** © 2007 Matt Brett, All Rights Reserved
p. 143 **http://lacuria.commovieworld** Carlos E. Subero © 2007
p. 143 **http://www.firewheeldesign.com** © 2007 Firewheel Design, Inc.
p. 143 **http://www.notonlybutalso.net** Not Only But Also © 2007
p. 144 **http://www.myvirb.com**
p. 144 **http://ignition360.co.uk** Stewart Bradford © 2007
p. 144 **http://www.fullyillustrated.com** Michael Heald © 2007
p. 144 **http://www.buzzrecruitment.co.nz** Meta Solutions © 2007
p. 144 **http://coda.co.za/** Damien du Toit © 2007
p. 145 **http://www.strife.dk** Michael Nielsen © 2007
p. 145 **http://26bits.com** 26bits © 2007 Chris Wilson
p. 147 **http://www.snappages.com** SnapPages © 2007
p. 147 **http://www.accessibilityinfocus.co.uk** Duncan Stevenson and John Stewart © 2007
p. 147 **http://www.wallcandyart.co.uk** Wallcandy Art Ltd © 2007
p. 147 **http://www.craigarmstrongonline.com** Adam Lloyd © 2007
p. 147 **http://www.tomas-design.com** Tomas Ledba © 2007
p. 148 **http://www.jigobite.com** Leon Hong © 2007
p. 148 **http://www.deardorffinc.com** Deardorff Communications © 2007
p. 148 **http://www.ronniesan.com** ©2007 by Ronnie Garcia
p. 148 **http://www.leakingmind.com** Rolando Rubalcava © 2007
p. 150 **http://coudal.com** © 2007 Coudal Partners, Inc.
p. 150 **http://www.mindfour.com** © 2007 MindFour. All Rights Reserved.
p. 150 **http://www.mstefan.comblog** Markus Stefan © 2007
p. 150 **http://www.vectorian.de** © 2007
p. 150 **http://www.workgroup.ie** Conor & David © 2007
p. 151 **http://www.limedesign.co.nz/** Lime Design © 2007
p. 151 **http://www.bbdata.ca** Jeffrey Li © 2006
p. 151 **http://www.itchypixel.net** Daniel Sarkozy © 2007
p. 151 **http://www.tskdesign.ro** Razvan Caliman © 2006
p. 152 **http://justice.anglican.org.nz** The Social Justice Commission of the Anglican Church in Aotearoa, New Zealand and Polynesia © 2007
p. 153 **http://perso.orange.frpixeldragon/portfolio5/** Julien Eichinger © 2007
p. 153 **http://www.clearwired.com** Clearwired Web Services, LLC © 2007
p. 153 **http://www.digitalwellbeing.eu/dwb** dwb © 2007
p. 153 **http://www.frzi.com** © 2007 Freek Zijlmans
p. 153 **http://www.cocoatech.com** Cocoatech © 2007
p. 154 **http://www.playgroundpilot.com** © andy widodo. playgroundpilot. 2006
p. 154 **http://www.pauljohns.com** Paul Johns © 2007
p. 154 **http://www.pixelgarten.de** pixelgarten / catrin altenbrandt & adrian niessler © 2007
p. 154 **http://www.m1k3.net** © 2007 Michael Dick
p. 154 **http://www.hyperisland.se** Hyper Island © 2007
p. 155 **http://www.onebyone.com.au** onebyone © 2007

p. 155 **http://www.peterpixel.nl** peterpixel © 2007
p. 157 **http://www.blond-kassel.de** PLUSX.de © 2007
p. 157 **http://www.pulpcards.co.uk** pulp © 2007
p. 157 **http://www.mindmeister.com** © 2007 by Codemart GmbH
p. 157 **http://gtc.td-webdesign.se** © Mattias Hagberg, Lisma.se © 2007
p. 157 **http://www.atomplastic.com** Atom Plastic © 2005
p. 158 **http://www.teaandcrumpets.org** Tea and Crumpets © 2007
p. 158 **http://www.fakefrench.com** Fake French © 2004-2007
p. 158 **http://www.pinksandblues.com** Pinks & Blues © 2007
p. 158 **http://www.puccipetwear.com** Puchi Petwear © 2007
p. 160 **http://thechoppr.com** TheChoppr © 2007
p. 160 **http://www.watertankco.com.au** Watertankco © 2007
p. 160 **http://www.nicolekidd.com** Nicole Kidd © 2007
p. 160 **http://www.tweakcast.com** Fallout Media © 2007
p. 161 **http://www.hellomedia.com.au** Hello Media © 2007
p. 161 **http://iconkits.com** © Bombia Design AB (Incorporated)
p. 161 **http://www.hbcweb.com** Copyright © 2007 - HBCWeb. com - All Rights Reserved
p. 161 **http://www.creixems.comeng** Jaime Creixems - Creixems Web Studio © 2007
p. 161 **http://www.flippingpad.com** Big In Europe, LLC © 2007
p. 162 **http://www.professionalontheweb.com** Extendi © 2007
p. 162 **http://www.uncover.com** Copyright © 2007 Uncover, LLC
p. 164 **http://www.amdesign.com** AM Design © 2007
p. 164 **http://www.carbonmade.com** nterface, LLC © 2005
p. 164 **http://www.danielpospisil.cz** Daniel Pospíšil © 2007
p. 164 **http://www.smallpositives.com** SmallPositives © 2007
p. 164 **http://www.swaroopch.com** Swaroop C H © 2007
p. 164 **http://wp-themes.designdisease.com** Design Disease © 2007
p. 164 **http://www.nterface.com** nterface, LLC © 2007
p. 165 **http://www.sitemost.com.au** SiteMost Pty Ltd © 2007
p. 165 **http://www.stargraphicdesign.com** Jessica Sykes © 2007
p. 165 **http://www.citricox.com** Citricox © 2006
p. 165 **http://www.hexabomb.com** Hexabomb Studios © 2007
p. 166 **http://www.lanico.hr** Lanico d.o.o. © 2007
p. 166 **http://www39design.com** 939 Design © 2007
p. 168 **http://www.luckyoliver.com** © 2007 LuckyOliver & MegaGlobal Image Syndicate, Inc.
p. 168 **http://www.aarronwalter.com** Aarron Walter © 2007
p. 168 **http://styleboost.com** Johan Bakken © 2007
p. 168 **http://www.survivingthepixel.com** © Catherine Davenport 2007. All rights reserved.
p. 168 **http://www.mostpreviewed.com** Copyright © Most Previewed. Built by Mubashar Iqbal over at Suffolk Software. Designed by Climax
p. 169 **http://www.jamiegregory.co.uk** Jamie Gregory © 2007
p. 169 **http://www.lancewyman.com** © 2005 by Lance Wyman
p. 169 **http://shop.tokyocube.com** Tokyocube © 2007
p. 169 **http://www.antilimit.com** Eric M Gustafson © 2007
p. 169 **http://www.frosk.org** frosk.org © 2007
p. 170 **http://www.effect.ie** Effect Design © 2007
p. 170 **http://www.serph.com** Advantage Consulting Services, Inc. © 2007
p. 170 **http://www.nypocreative.co.uk** Andrew Butterworth © 2007
p. 173 **http://www.elixirgraphics.com** elixir graphics © 2007
p. 173 **http://www.cropix.ru** © 2007 ООО Инстинкт мастерства, © 2007 pajasu
p. 173 **http://www.e-junkie.com** 19 Degrees © 2007
p. 173 **http://www.ripple.org** ripple.org © 2007
p. 174 **http://www.elementfusion.com** ElementFusion © 2007
p. 174 **http://www.igeeks.org** iGeeks © 2007
p. 174 **http://resolio.com** Resolio © 2007

p. 174 **http://www.splitdivision.com** SplitDivision © 2007 All rights reserved.
p. 175 **http://kevadamson.comtalking-of-design** Kev Adamson © 2007
p. 175 **http://www.nclud.comsketchbook** nclud LLC © 2007
p. 176 **http://www.riverfrontpark.com** Riverfront Park © 2007
p. 176 **http://www.avenuegc.co.uk** Avenue Graphical Communication © 2007
p. 176 **http://alexsancho.name** Alex Sancho © 2005
p. 176 **http://www.squible.com** Theron Parlin © 2007
p. 176 **http://www.anderswahlberg.comblogg** Anders Wahlberg, Sweden © 2007
p. 176 **http://www.newearthonline.co.uk** David G. Paul © 2007
p. 177 **http://www.scottsaw.com** Scott Saw Art © 2007
p. 177 **http://www.us.mobaito.com** deahna © 2007
p. 177 **http://www.leandaryan.com** Leanda Ryan © 2007
p. 178 **http://www.440media.com** 2440 Media, Inc. © 2007
p. 178 **http://www.dtelepathy.com** digital-telepathy © 2007
p. 178 **http://www.scriggleit.com** Blackwood Media Group © 2007
p. 178 **http://lifelike.se** Lifelike AB © 2007
p. 179 **http://www.ungarbage.com** Mourylise Heymer Marreiros © 2007
p. 179 **http://www.mattinglydesign.net** mattinglydesign.net © 2007
p. 180 **http://webstruments.com** Copyright © 2001-2007 Webstruments
p. 180 **http://www.mrwebhead.com** mrwebhead.com © 2007
p. 180 **http://www.luisalarcon.comblog** Luis Alarcón© 2007
p. 180 **http://www.teresawalsh.com** Teresa Walsh © 2007
p. 180 **http://www.silverorange.com** silverorange Inc. © 2007
p. 181 **http://royalevibes.com** Karel-Jan Vercruysse l EenOntwerper.be © 2007
p. 182 **http://guilago.se** Guilago © 2007
p. 182 **http://www.elan3.com** Timothy J Sears © 2007
p. 182 **http://www.djtimbo.com** DJ Timbo © 2006
p. 182 **http://www.bio-bak.nl** Coen Grift © 2007
p. 183 **http://www.antidecaf.com** Anders Johnsen / antidecaf. com © 2007
p. 183 **http://incrediblebox.com** © Incredible Box
p. 183 **http://www.samcreate.comblog** samcreate © 2007
p. 183 **http://fluxility.com** Fluxility Design © 2006-2007
p. 183 **http://www.interestingfacts.org** InterestingFacts.org © 2007
p. 185 **http://www.bigsweaterdesign.com** Vincent Maglione © 2007
p. 185 **http://www.simonestudio.com** SimoneStudio © 2007
p. 185 **http://www.rebeccapaterson.co.uk** artwork by Rebecca Paterson, design and development Binary Vein Digital Media © 2007
p. 185 **http://www.gospodicna.si** fulspectrum media © 2007
p. 185 **http://www.flyingturtle.net** Flying Turtle Studio © 2007
p. 186 **http://www.okb.es** okb estudio interactivo © 2007
p. 186 **http://www.outline2design.com** Perflect Corporation © 2007
p. 186 **http://www.swiths.com** swiths.com © 2005
p. 188 **http://www.smallfarmdesign.com** Small Farm Design © 2007
p. 188 **http://waetzigdesign.com** WaetzigDesign©2007
p. 188 **http://www.alexswanson.netblog** AlexSwanson.net © 2007
p. 188 **http://www.golfmedic.net** Golfmedic.net © 2007
p. 188 **http://www.joinradius.com** Joinradius.com © 2007
p. 188 **http://www.factioninc.com** Factioninc.com © 2007
p. 189 **http://contrabrand.net** brandon todd wilson © 2007
p. 189 **http://www.djdynamike.com** Michael Nagy © 2007

p. 189 **http://www.loicsans.com** loicsans© 2007
p. 189 **http://pixelfly.net** Martin Aglas © 2007
p. 190 **http://www.simonwiffen.co.uk** Simon Wiffen © 2007
p. 190 **http://www.jasonlarosedesign.com** © 2007 Jason LaRose
p. 191 **http://www.saturdate.org** Cody Smith © 2007
p. 191 **http://www.brandempire.com** Duncan Robertson © 2007
p. 191 **http://plushie.avocadolite.com** avocadolite © 2007
p. 191 **http://www.merix.com.pl** Copyright © MERIX 2006
p. 191 **http://www.dolphincruises.co.nz/** InterCity Group (NZ) Ltd © 2007
p. 192 **http://www.dabhand.pl** Dab Hand Studio © 2007
p. 192 **http://www.webleeddesign.com** © 2007 Bryan Katzel
p. 193 **http://www.firstflash.net** Firstflash X-media Labor, Hamburg © 2007
p. 193 **http://www.michaelcourier.com** Michael Alan Courier © 2007
p. 194 **http://www.notcot.org** NOTCOT Inc © 2007
p. 194 **http://www.copious.co.uk** Copious Ltd © 2007
p. 194 **http://www.errolschwartz.com** Errol Schwartz © 2007
p. 194 **http://www.hakustyle.com** abejin © 2007
p. 194 **http://www.bouroullec.com** Ronan & Erwan Bouroullec © 2007
p. 195 **http://www.distancemedia.co.uk** David Emery © 2007
p. 195 **http://www.upstairsmarketing.com** Upstairs Marketing Group © 2004
p. 195 **http://www.casperelectronics.com** © 2007 Ryan Masuga, Masuga Design
p. 195 **http://run.likethewind.ca** Fathima Cader © 2007
p. 196 **http://www.digitalkick.com** © 2007 DigitalKick
p. 196 **http://www.brainfood.com** Brainfood.com © 2007
p. 197 **http://www.berenguer.info** Joaquim Berenguer © 2007
p. 197 **http://www.fishbond.net** Petr Skopal © 2007
p. 197 **http://www.alexanderwalter.com** Alexander Walter © 2005
p. 197 **http://www.amberbowe.com** Amber Bowe © 2007
p. 198 **http://www.snowsuit.net** Ryan Keberly © 2007
p. 198 **http://www.cabanadigital.com** Cabana Digital © 2007
p. 198 **http://www.matthew-design.com** Matthew Design © 2007
p. 199 **http://photomatt.net** Matt Mullenweg © 2007
p. 200 **http://dailyminefield.com** Patrick Craig © 2007
p. 200 **http://www.cameronmoll.com** Cameron Moll © 2007
p. 200 **http://www.aftercode.com** aftercode © 2007
p. 200 **http://www.hansthedouble.com** Justin Lerner © 2007
p. 201 **http://www.factory4.co.uk** FactoryFour © 2007
p. 201 **http://www4-7media.de** 247 Media Studios © 2007
p. 201 **http://www.jindraholy.info** Jindra Holy © 2007
p. 201 **http://www.digitalemon.com** Digitalemon © 2006
p. 203 **http://www.nitram-nunca.com** Kei Sasaki © 2007
p. 203 **http://www.pioneer10.com** Copyright © Duane King
p. 203 **http://www.purevolume.com** © 2007 Copyright Virb Inc. All Rights Reserved
p. 203 **http://www.hopkingdesign.com** Mez Hopking © MMVII
p. 203 **http://www.kqed.orgquest** KQED © 2007
p. 204 **http://www.nonstop.tv/silver/** NonStop Television AB © 2007
p. 204 **http://www.lealea.net** Copyright © Lealea Design. All Rights Reserved.
p. 204 **http://payplay.fm** PayPlay © 2007
p. 206 **http://www.csstux.com** elixir graphics © 2007
p. 206 **http://www.defrost.ca** Defrost Design Works Inc. © 2007
p. 206 **http://arch-enemy.net** Arch Enemy Entertainment © 2006-2007

p. 206 **http://www.talkxbox.com** TalkXbox.com © 2007
p. 207 **http://www.kloobik.org** Frédéric Viau - kloobik.org © 2007
p. 207 **http://www.egolounge.de** Enrico Müller © 2007
p. 207 **http://www.shape5.com** Shape 5 © 2007
p. 208 **http://www.tamberlow.com** Max Bassani - Tamberlow snc © 2007
p. 208 **http://www.bkanal.ch/** orange8 interactive ag © 2007
p. 211 **http://graphictherapy.com** David Calderley © 2007
p. 211 **http://handmadeinteractive.comjasonlove** © Jason Love 2007
p. 212 **http://www.rickycox.com** © Copyright: Ricky Cox, 2007
p. 212 **http://www.webfellowforhire.com** Richard McCoy © 2007
p. 212 **http://www.miguelperez.es** Miguel Pérez © 2007
p. 212 **http://www.bluevertigo.com.ar** Blue Vertigo © 2007
p. 213 **http://www.mutanz.com** Cesar Jacobi © 2007
p. 213 **http://www.peter-hermann.com** Peter Hermann © 2007
p. 213 **http://www.neu-e.de** David Hofmann // boxdoodle.com © 2007
p. 214 **http://www.jlern.com** Justin Lerner © 2007
p. 215 **http://www.caravanpictures.com** Caravan Pictures © 2007
p. 215 **http://www.matthewmahon.com** © Matthew Mahon 2007
p. 216 **http://www.javierferrervidal.com** javierferrervidal© 2007
p. 216 **http://www.sofake.com** Jordan Stone © 2002
p. 217 **http://www.thebathwater.com** thebathwater.com © 2007
p. 217 **http://www.exponentialdesign.co.uk** Clemens Hackl Design © 2007
p. 218 **http://www.themillbank.com** The Millbank © 2007
p. 218 **http://www.conceptm.nl** Concept M © 2007
p. 218 **http://www.azuna.net** AZUNA, LLC© 2007
p. 219 **http://www.xrs.pl** xrs nowe media © 2007
p. 219 **http://www.gullyland.com** gully © 2006
p. 221 **http://www.webdesign20.com** Web Design 2.0 © 2007
p. 221 **http://www.lmdesign.net** Light Motion Design © 2007
p. 221 **http://www.mandchou.com** mandchou © 2007
p. 222 **http://www.hmtmx.com** Ho-Man Tin Music © 2007
p. 222 **http://a-i.tw/** All Right reserved by Ai Interactive Media © 2007
p. 223 **http://www.studio-stemmler.com** stemmler © 2007
p. 223 **http://casestudies.labforculture.org** FONDAZIONE FITZCARRALDO © 2006
p. 224 **http://www.praguedesign.cz** Katerina Pekna, Pavel Moravec © 2007
p. 224 **http://newsberry.com** Wildbit, LLC © 2007
p. 225 **http://esopusmag.com** Esopus Foundation Ltd. © 2007
p. 225 **http://www.valentinaolini.com** Valentina Olini (www.valentinaolini.com) © 2007 - All Right Reserved
p. 225 **http://www.babytoothcenter.com** descom© 2007
p. 225 **http://sarajoypond.com** SaraJoyPond © 2007
p. 225 **http://www.netresults.com** NetResults, LLC © 2007
p. 225 **http://rebusiness.com.au** ReBusiness © 2007
p. 227 **http://www.mochiads.com** Mochi Media, Inc. © 2007
p. 227 **http://www.ocean70.com** oceanseventy © 2007
p. 227 **http://business-paper.dk** Thomas Fals - Retouch ApS © 2007
p. 227 **http://www.nemarkmedia.co.uk** nemark media © 2007
p. 227 **http://www.habitat.orgyouthprograms** Habitat for Humanity International © 2007
p. 228 **http://www.orbitshakers.com** Orbit Shakers © 2007
p. 228 **http://pdim.net** © 2007 Progressive Design In Motion
p. 228 **http://www.koder.cz** Petr Vagner © 2007
p. 228 **http://www.mailandgo.co.uk** in2 © 2007
p. 230 **http://www.entertainmentafrica.com** Copyright © 2007 EntertainmentAfrica.com

p. 230 **http://www.havocstudios.co.uk** Havoc Studios © 2007 - Ryan Taylor & Paul Stanton
p. 230 **http://www.listentomanchester.co.uk** Copyright © 2003-2008 ListenNOW. All rights reserved.
p. 230 **http://www.churchmedia.cc** Church Media Group, Inc. © 2007
p. 231 **http://www.gagles.com.br** gagles © 2007
p. 231 **http://www.frankfurt.de** © Stadt Frankfurt am Main 2007
p. 231 **http://www.blacktomato.co.uk** Black Tomato © 2007
p. 232 **http://www.nicolashuon.info** Nicolas Huon © 2007
p. 232 **http://www.sushibeads.com** Hoi-Lun Chiu © 2007
p. 233 **http://www.pocketwebsite.net** 2007 © Bosq.Net
p. 233 **http://www.espaciozero.com** EspacioZero Etchevarne. net © 2007
p. 233 **http://www.tolgaerbay.com** tolgaerbay© 2007
p. 233 **http://www.creativeireland.com** creativeireland © 2007
p. 233 **http://workbench-music.com** Sébastien Marchal © 2007
p. 233 **http://audicted.de** Jan Weiss © 2007
p. 235 **http://www.didoo.net** Area Web © 2007
p. 235 **http://www.nickdeakin.com** Nick Deakin © 2007
p. 235 **http://anatolip.com** Anatoli Papirovski © 2007
p. 236 **http://www.retrostrobe.com** retrostrobe* © 2007
p. 236 **http://www.booreiland.nl** © 2007 Booreiland
p. 236 **http://lukestevensdesign.com** Luke Stevens © 2007
p. 236 **http://www.sromek.cz** Sromek.cz © 2007
p. 236 **http://brivilati.com** Jorge Brivilati © 2007
p. 237 **http://www.philippseifried.com** Philipp Seifried © 2007
p. 237 **http://www.grondecki.pl/portfolio.html** Łukasz Grondecki © 2007
p. 237 **http://www.laksman.com.ar** Martin Laksman © 2007
p. 237 **http://www.allankirsten.com** Allan Kirsten © 2007
p. 237 **http://www.ryanjclose.com** Ryan Close © 2007
p. 238 **http://www.dougdosberg.com** Doug Dosberg © 2007
p. 238 **http://www.touristr.com** Tourist Republic © 2007
p. 239 **http://sis.slowli.com** © 2007 Stefan Sicher, Switzerland
p. 239 **http://www.larissameek.com** Larissa Meek © 2007
p. 239 **http://www.asfusion.com** AsFusion © 2007
p. 239 **http://businesslogs.com** Forty © 2007
p. 239 **http://www.elliotswan.com** Elliot Swan © 2007
p. 239 **http://www.vagrantradio.com** Copyright © 2007 Jason Scott Pant
p. 241 **http://www.vtks.com.br** vtks © 2007
p. 241 **http://www.zeppenfeld.com** www.excite-bremen.de, www.quadrifolia.de © 2007
p. 241 **http://www.moodboard.com** moodboard © 2007
p. 241 **http://www.bigsquaredot.com** © 2007 Big Square Dot
p. 242 **http://www.trout.com.au** Trout Creative Thinking 2007
p. 242 **http://www.koehorstintveld.nl** Koehorst in 't Veld © 2007
p. 242 **http://www.michaelfakesch.com** Itisblank © 2007
p. 242 **http://tinyteam.com** Tiny Team © 2007
p. 244 **http://www.digitalmash.com** Rob Morris © 2007
p. 244 **http://www.bensaunders.com** Ben Saunders © 2007
p. 244 **http://www.dogoworld.free.fr** Mamzhell.Dogo © 2007
p. 244 **http://www.iris-interactive.fr** IRIS Interactive © 2007
p. 245 **http://accent.free.fr** Axel Antoine © 2007
p. 245 **http://www.its.com.uy** Copiright: Infrastructure Technology Services© 2007
p. 245 **http://www.brandneusense.com** Helen Campbell © 2007
p. 245 **http://www.novalux.com** Novalux, Inc. © 2007
p. 245 **http://anniesgourmetkitchen.net** Graphic D-Signs, Inc. © 2007